KEITH SCOTT

A Time Place for Healing

Kravitz & Sons

INNOVATORS IN PUBLISHING MARKETING AND ADVERTISING

Kravitz and Sons LLC
204 E Arlington Blvd. Suite B
Greenville, NC 27858

Published by Kravitz and Sons LLC.

ISBN: 979-8-89639-352-8 (sc)
ISBN: 979-8-89639-351-1 (e)
ISBN: 979-8-89639-368-9 (hb)

Library of Congress Control Number: 2025915549

Table of Contents

PREFACE

I would like to dedicate this book to those in need of a goal in life, to all those who are lost and feel hopeless. We too often look down at people struggling with emotional issues or those we call down and out. We are quick to judge and label them without really knowing them or what they have gone through. Thousands or war veterans and homeless and thousands of others have ended their lives due to depression. Hundreds or thousands of our children suffer emotional issues, and we lose thousands of them needlessly every year. We can all help with just a little understanding and love, and by doing so, we can understand and help ourselves. I dedicate this book to those looking for help as well as those not looking but need it. I also dedicate it to those doing their best to make a difference.

Chapter 1

Building a New Life

Alderwood was a small town of less than thirty-five thousand people. It was a rural community nestled in a small valley surrounded by small mountains on three sides. Streams from the surrounding terrain flowed together to merge into a small river that flowed through town. There was only one main road into town at one end. There were small unimproved dirt roads that led up into the mountains to lakes, camping sites, and other wilderness areas at the other end of town. The town got its name because of the abundance of trees surrounding the town which were mostly alder. Several other varieties of trees, however, included pines, oak, maple, birch, as well as others. It made for thickly forested surroundings on the hillsides.

This was one of the main reasons Roger had decided to move here, along with the fact that the town was in a secluded area and, for the most part, very quiet. He had found his house, which was at the edge of town with the back of the property adjacent to the trees and hillside. It was rather run-down, in pretty bad condition, and had been vacant for several years. The bank, which had foreclosed on it, was anxious to sell it at a reasonable price. It was the perfect location and size for Roger, however, and he went to the bank manager with an offer. He found out that it had been vacant so long and was so old it had been condemned. To move in, it would have to be fixed up to meet the building codes. It would take a lot of major improvements before he could occupy the place. At the time, Roger had a small motor home and asked if he could park it on the property and live in it while he made the improvements.

Darrell, the bank manager, said, "If we can come up with reasonable price, I would be glad to get it off our hands. However, it would take a lot of work to bring it up to code. Are you sure you are up to the task?"

"I'm pretty handy with tools and have done a fair amount of remodeling in my time. In fact, I carry a large assortment of woodworking tools at all times since it is my hobby."

"We'll have to check with Bob to go ahead."

"Who is Bob?"

"Oh, he is the mayor. As a small community, we usually go by first names, and things are handled informally here. He also takes care of the housing and development. He and I went to school together, and we usually can handle matters with a phone call and take care of any paperwork later. I'll give him a call right now."

Darrell picked up the phone and made the call.

"Hello, Bob. Remember that property on Oak Avenue that we talked about the other day that has been condemned? I have a gentleman here who is interested in buying it. He says he is willing to fix it up to meet required codes before moving in. He has a motor home that he wants to park on the property and live in until he can move in. His name is Roger. Here, let me put us on speaker so we all can join in."

"Hi, Roger, I hear you would like to purchase a piece of property in our little community?"

Roger replied, "That is right. It is perfect for my needs."

"Well, Roger, what is your last name?"

"I just go by Roger."

"We can take care of that when we get to signing the paperwork. Well, as I was saying, maybe Darrell neglected to give you the complete lowdown concerning the property. It was one of the first structures built in our town and, as such, has been designated as a historical site. That means the exterior cannot be altered without approval from the historical society. That, along with bringing it up to code for modern living, could be a challenging task."

"I have no intention of changing anything on the outside. I like the house as it stands, and I also like the outbuildings. I am willing to do what has to be done to make it livable and up to code."

Darrell now cut in, "Bob, I can vouch for Roger, and we have gone over the financial issue. When we finalize the agreement, we will use full legal names."

Bob's reply was delayed a little, but he finally replied, "Roger, I have no problem going by first names, and as Darrell, I'm sure, has already told you, here we usually go on first name basis. Since Darrell says he can vouch for you and has assured me full legal names will appear on all documents, I have no problem. It sounds as if you bought yourself a house. Welcome to Alderwood."

"Thank you, Bob," Darrell said. "Remember our golf date on Sunday. You better bring your A game. See you then." And he hung up.

He then turned to Roger. "Well, that was relatively easy, but we have some paperwork to get to, and we can get the power turned on. Considering all the work you will be doing, I feel the price we discussed earlier is fair. And if you still agree, we can get you signed up for a loan here at the bank at a real reasonable rate."

"No loan," Rogers replied. "I will pay cash."

"You don't possibly carry that much cash with you, do you?"

"No, but if you want to call my bank, we can arrange to have them send you a cashier's check for the full amount as soon as possible. And, by the way, since I will be living here, I will need a local bank to take over my finances. Can you recommend one?" Of course, he was jesting. He already had decided to transfer his funds to Darrell's bank.

He just wanted to get a reaction. He then smiled at Darrell, and they both had a good-natured laugh.

Being the bank president as well as owner, it made things a lot easier. However, the bank lawyer would have to look over everything to make sure it was all legal. They did get on the phone with Roger's bank, and to Darrell's shock, the transfer of funds in the full amount was no problem. In a couple of hours, everything was completed, signed, and notarized. They opened a new account at the bank with an agreement to have the rest of his assets transferred. After a handshake, other niceties, and another welcome to the community, Roger was on his way to his new home.

Chapter 2

Making a New Home

Roger, although not young, in his early to midseventies, was a hard worker. He was a jack of all trades, having advanced skills in many areas. He had a trailer that he pulled behind his motor home full of power as well as hand tools. The property already had an open garage at the back of the house which became his workshop. Behind that was a small barn, and another small shed was at the back on the other side of the property. There was a coral attached to the barn, and the property extended into the woods at a slight slope behind his place. These features were the reason for his selection of the property. It was ideal for his purposes.

None of the buildings were in great shape, but they were sound, especially the house. But being built over a hundred years ago, the plumbing and electrical were outdated. Plumbing was something he was familiar with and could handle, but the electrical would require a licensed electrician. Everything would just take time, and he had to get started.

The house had a front and back porch that were covered. The back porch extended all the way from one side of the house to a room attached behind the house on the other side. A door went to the kitchen, and another went into the room from the porch. From that room, another door opened up into the garage, making it a perfect storage and workroom for his tools. The rest of the house was a square shape. The door from the back porch opened into the kitchen. To the left of the kitchen from the back was a bedroom, and in front of that was a bathroom which needed major work. The living room took up the rest of the house. It was separated from kitchen by a wall with an open doorway. It extended from one side of the house to the other with a window on the front wall and one on each side. A fireplace was in the corner of the wall separating the kitchen and wall adjacent to the driveway. The driveway, which was dirt mixed with gravel, led to the back of the house and garage with parking in the back. The front door opened on to a small porch with five steps down into the lawn which was about thirty feet deep and fifty feet wide. Overgrown shrubbery encircled the whole property except in the back where it went into the woods. There was a picket fence that also enclosed the property except for the open driveway but was almost impossible to see because of the vegetation. You could make out roses within the plants and weed, but it would take a lot of work to trim and weed them.

The outside, however, would have to wait. Roger had to take care of work in the house so he could move in. He soon was using the trailer, making trips to the local hardware store, lumberyard, junkyard—any place he could find to procure what was needed. Being a private person, he never asked for help, nor did he hire anyone to help except for the electrical work. He did everything else by himself. Life started early each day, and he worked well into the night. He only had one outlet for electrical purposes, so he had to work by lamplight after dark.

Soon the house started looking pretty good, at least on the inside. From the outside, little improvement was noticeable. But that was not a requirement to move in or pass building codes. Soon he was able to move in with all inspections passed and codes met.

Since the house and property had been run-down and vacant so long, neighborhood children came to consider it haunted. Since the grade school and junior high were only a couple of blocks away and were on the same street as his house, several children passed by each day. Roger was doing almost all work inside, and since his motor home and trailer were parked in the back, out of sight, they never realized someone had moved in. But when they started seeing lights in the house and shadows moving about, their belief in a haunted house theory was intensified.

For personal needs, such as groceries and other shopping, he did it at night to avoid contact with other people. He used the twenty- four-hour stores. This contributed to theory of a haunted house because no one saw him during the day, especially the children. The runs he had to make for material was usually while the children were in school. He always parked in the back of the house, out of sight from the road. He just wanted to maintain his privacy, and he knew children were not only the most curious but the most mischievous. His banker and the mayor were the only ones who knew who he was and that he had bought the house.

Within two months, he had made the improvements necessary to meet codes and pass inspections, which meant he was able to move in. Windows were repaired, all electrical updated, all new plumbing fixtures installed, and all other plumbing updated. There were other inside improvements he wanted to make, but everything necessary for his moving in was accomplished.

Next on his list was the barn and property behind the house. These needed to be repaired, and the garage needed to be cleaned out to make room for his trailer. He also planned to sell the motor home now that it was no longer needed and buy a pickup that he could pull the trailer with and haul larger items. He also wanted to buy a goat for milk and chickens for eggs, and the coral and barn needed repair to accommodate them. His goal was to become as independent as possible. He needed the truck and trailer to transport them and their feed. He also planned to buy wheat and grind it to make his own flour. Bees were also on his list. And a garden would provide most everything needed to reach that goal. He enjoyed cooking and canning, and the fruit trees would also provide for food storage as well as providing food for the animals. With the proper use and care of what he could provide, he figured one trip a month for spices and other minor items would be sufficient.

So the barn, coral, and other outbuildings now became his center of attention. He had already contacted a farmer who raised goats and arranged to purchase a young female with a kid and was producing milk. He had to wait for the kid to be old enough to be separated before picking up the nanny, which would be about a week. He also was going to get about a dozen chickens from the same famer at the same time. Luckily, he was able to find a beekeeper in the area that he could purchase a queen and some bees from. The hive he would place on the back of his property at the tree line. There was a lot to prepare for his animals, but they were critical to his way of life. The chickens would be in a separate fenced-in area next to the coral where the goat would be able to reside with an area inside the barn for her.

The other storage shed would be used for storage of tools and woods as he was a woodworker and planned to harvest raw hardwood from the forest behind his property. These would be used in planned projects in the future.

He managed to trade in the motor home for a used pickup. It was not fancy but ran well, and the trade didn't cost him a dime. The dealer, in fact, was very pleased with the trade.

Another two weeks and he was ready to welcome his new residents to the property. They would become his family, and he treated them as such. The goat he named Nanny—not very original, but names did not matter to him, and it was easy to remember.

Now he was prepared to paint the house and work on the fence once he cleared away the weeds. This project would have to be done delicately because his property, being on a street frequented by schoolchildren, posed a situation he wanted to avoid. He knew his appearance would create rumors and possible situations he wanted to avoid. He knew his appearance was not the standard. He had long hair and a beard, and his clothes were worn and out of style. To be honest, he looked like a tramp. For this reason, he worked on the front of his property after they were in school and before they were let out. Fortunately, the bushes and overgrown roses hid him from the sidewalk and street traffic for the most part.

Two years into his residency, the front was still in poor condition. He had maintained his privacy and concentrated his efforts on the care of his animals and improvements in the house and the property behind it. He had put in a garden and, by all standards, kept a proper barnyard. However, the front yard still needed a lot of work. He had transformed the storage next to the back porch into a workshop and spent hours in there working on his woodworking projects. But he had neglected the front. Working in the lawn was not his cup of tea.

Chapter 3

Liza

There was a park less than a block from Roger's place on the same street. There were only three other properties between his property and the park. The park was right next to the grade school. Children often played in the park after school before going home. It was late summer, and Roger decided to work in the front after the schoolchildren had gone home for the day since there would still be a lot of daylight left. He waited for about half an hour, and when he thought the children had moved past, he went out to do his least liked chores. About a half hour into his weeding, trimming, and cleaning up, he heard a group of children in front of his property creating a fuss. He had been engrossed in his project and didn't see them coming up the walk. A group of about six had stayed to play in the park and were now headed home later than he expected.

He immediately halted his activity in fear they would hear him. If he stayed still and made no noise, he was sure they would not notice him behind all the shrubbery. He was aware of the reputation his place had, especially among the younger residents, and he didn't want to create a scene.

The uproar became louder. He heard a young girl crying profusely. He heard "ga, ga, garbage g-girl" over and over again.

Finally he heard the girl of about ten respond, "St-st-stop it, st-st-stop it." She was crying out of control with her hands over her face and had dropped her books on the walk.

They, or at least some, continued to taunt her, "Ga, ga, garbage g- g-girl."

He could not take it anymore. He knew what it was like to be made fun of for being different. He stood up, and immediately, everyone began screaming and running away—all except one. The young girl who was so upset, with her hands over her eyes, crying so hard she never noticed anything. No wonder they ran. Out of the bushes stepped a figure with a long white beard, a straw hat, torn, ragged coveralls and gloves on his hands, holding shears in one hand and a small garden shovel in the other.

He put down his tools, walked over to the girl, giving her a big hug. "Now, now, they are gone now. Everything will be all right.

She was still crying and wasn't able to see much, especially since she was in such a close embrace. She couldn't see who was holding her. "N-no it w-will n-never be all-all right."

"Now, now, it may seem like that now, but things get better. Why were they teasing you and calling you that name?"

"M-my father is a ga garbage man, and, and the way I t-talk."

"There is nothing wrong with being a sanitation engineer. Without them we would all be covered in trash. It is a very important and noble profession. You should be proud of him. And as far as the way you talk, there is nothing to be ashamed of. We all have our challenges."

At that, she pulled herself back a little and he knelt down, pulled a handkerchief from his pocket, and started drying her tears away. As soon as she could see clearly, she stepped back a little further in fear and looked him over. "Who-who are y-you and w-where did y- you come from? Are y-you going to h-hurt me?"

"No, I would never hurt you. My name is Roger, and this is my place. May I inquire as to the name of this beautiful young lady standing before me?"

"I-I'm not su-supposed to t-talk to st-strangers. A-and I am n-not be-beautiful."

"Well, I think you are very beautiful, but I don't think beautiful is your name. So, beautiful, do you have another name, or shall I just call you beautiful?"

"You t-talk funny."

"Well, I guess we have that in common. Now let's get you cleaned up, and you can calm down, and I will call your folks to pick you up, beautiful."

"No, y-you can't c-call my p-parents. And my n-name is Liza, not b- beautiful."

"Now why can't we call your parents? They will be worried about you."

"W-we just c-can't. Are y-you a g-ghost?"

"No, I am not a ghost, nor am I Santa Claus like some people think because I am so fat and have a long white beard. But I think you have to go home before your parents panic. I don't think you are in a condition to do it alone. I am sorry. I would walk you home, but I have another problem. I don't like to leave my home. Now let's go to the house. I have a batch of cookies I just made, and I'm sure we will figure things out."

Liza giggled a little at his Santa remark and by now has calmed down and was losing her fear of this strange new individual. He picked up his tools and her books, put them in one arm and put his other arm around Liza's shoulders, and led her up the driveway to the back of his house.

When they got back to the back porch, he sat her down on his swing that had a small table in front of it. "I'll be right back," he said.

He went into the house and shortly returned with a glass of milk and a plate of oatmeal cookies. He also had a wet cloth he used to wipe her face, which he proceeded to do.

"Now we can't have my princess looking like this. We have to get her presentable for her subjects."

Liza laughed again. "I am no pr princess, and I d-don't have su-subjects." Then she took a sip of milk. "This m-milk tastes f-funny, is it b-bad?"

"It is goat's milk. It comes from one of your subjects."

He then pointed to coral where Nanny was standing at the rail, bleating, "Na na na."

"Have you had goat's milk before? It is actually better for you than cow's milk."

"But it t-tastes f-funny."

"I know it takes a little getting used to, but once you do, you'll like it better than cow's milk. Now I think it is time to get in touch with your parents."

"But y-you can't t-tell them I h-have been c-crying or w-what happened."

"Y-you just c-can't or we w-will have to m-move again. I d-don't want to m-move again."

Roger could tell she was beginning to get very agitated again. "Okay, I won't mention it, but please give me the number so I can give them a call. I'll bring the phone out here so you can talk to them and provide what information you would like. However, lying is something I do not condone. I know if I got on the phone, there would be some questions neither of us are prepared to answer. We don't want them to get some wrong ideas or jump to conclusions."

He then brought out the phone that was on a long cord, set it down on the small table, and told her to dial home. "Hello, M-Mom. I'm s- sorry I am l late and d-didn't let y-you know. I-I stopped off a-at the park a-and lost t-track of t-time. Could y-you come d-down and w- walk me h-home? I am at a f-friend's house n-near the park, u-using the p-phone, but I can be th-there in a m-minute. I am a l-little tired a- and don't w-want to walk h-home alone. I'm s-sorry, I won't d-do it again."

Roger could hear her mother on the phone. "Where does your friend live? I can meet you there."

"N-no," Liza said. "I am s-so close t-to the p-park I will be th-there before y-you, and it w-would be too h-hard to t-tell you h-how to g- get here."

"I'll be there in ten minutes. That's about as soon as I can get there. I'll see you soon, honey, and we can talk when we get home." They then both hung up.

"Don't you have a car she can pick you up in?" asked Roger.

"W we have a c-car, but Dad h-has to use it to w-work."

"Well, you better get going so you will get there before her. Don't forget your books. You are welcome back anytime to visit your subjects, princess."

She gave him a little giggle and grabbed her books. They gave each other a big hug, and she sauntered down the driveway. She turned and gave him a wave, and he smiled and waved back.

Liza's family, the Petersons, had only moved to Alderwood a few months ago. Liza had not made any friends, and her and her family, so far, had not developed any relationships with anyone else in town. They had moved here primarily for Liza's sake. They came from a large city back East where she had been teased and pestered to the point that she refused to go to school. The school failed to recognize or do anything about the problem, and Scott and Jean, her parents, decided to move again. This had been their third move due to the recurring problem. Liza was the love of their lives since they found out they could have no more children, and both had experienced unpleasant or tragic upbringings themselves. Also, they had no other relatives that were known. This time they felt a move to the West to a small town may work. Having moved so much, her parents were struggling financially as well, unable to keep a job long enough to advance to a higher pay grade. Neither had a college degree, and things were tight. This was a move of desperation and a great risk. But for Liza's sake, they were willing to take it. Although they tried to keep the issue from her, she was completely aware of their sacrifice. It put a lot of pressure on her they weren't aware of, and she was determined to make things work. She was determined not to give her parents reason to move again.

Chapter 4

Nanny

The teasing of Liza after that day greatly diminished, at least on her trips home from school. Some of that was probably due to the fact Liza continued to walk on the side of the road that Roger's house was on, while the rest of the students avoided it like the plague, using the other side of the road. There were rumors and whispering at school but no outright harassment. Liza felt proud and held her head high because she was the brave one while everyone else was afraid of the haunted house and the monster that lived there. She now gained a sense of confidence she never had before. Besides, she had a new friend who liked her for who she was. Things were looking up. Her attitude was changing, and her parents noticed it. So it wasn't too big a surprise when she told her parents the next Friday she was going to visit a friend after school so would be a little late. A few of the other girls at school who had become friendly toward her questioned her on the incident that occurred the previous week. They asked her what happened that day and if the ghost had harmed her and if she was scared. She just replied saying she fought him off and she wasn't scared of him. Then she walked away with a smile on her face and her chin up. To some, she became a hero. To others, she was perceived as even stranger than before. Either way, she didn't care. She felt a sense of respect, and that was all that mattered.

With this new attitude, she turned into Roger's driveway after checking to see if anyone was looking. It was a beautiful Friday. As soon as she placed her books on the small table on the porch, she heard

Nanny bleating at the coral fence. "Na na na," she continued. Liza ran to her, petting her on the nose and head as Nanny stuck her head through the wooden fence. When Liza stopped petting her, Nanny began her "na na na" again.

"I don't think she will ever learn to say her whole name, but she keeps trying," Roger said from the porch."

Liza just laughed.

"You can get in the coral with her. Just go through the gate. She loves to play, and I don't have much time for her. She loves to play tag. But be careful when she tags you. It's a butt, and sometimes it can be a little energetic. She has knocked me over a couple of times. She also likes to be petted and rubbed down."

As Liza entered the pen, Roger said, "I didn't know if I would see you again, princess"

As she was holding Nanny around the neck, she replied, "I am not a p-princess."

"You are to me. Go ahead, start running. She will chase you, but be careful when she catches you. Then she'll want you to chase her. You'll tire long before she does, and when you're ready, I have some more cookies and milk, and we can talk a little."

Roger was right. By the time Liza was dragging, Nanny was rearing to go as ever with her usual "na na na." It was a greeting as well as a call for attention, with the latter probably 90 percent of the time.

As Liza gave her a big hug, she said, "I'm p-pooped. I'll p-play with you l-later. Bye."

Then she opened the gate and walked to the porch where Roger was sitting on the swing, watching her and Nanny as they played. "I told you she would wear you out. You were lucky. You didn't get knocked down once. She was gentle on you. Wait until next time. Here, have some cookies and milk and rest."

After she rested a little and had a cookie and took a sip of milk, she remarked, "I th-think I am g-getting used to this m-milk. It d- doesn't taste too b-bad."

"Don't let Nanny hear you say her milk doesn't taste too bad. She'll really give you a good butt. She thinks her milk is the greatest."

At that, Liza laughed and spit out milk and cookies as she did. Then Roger laughed, and they laughed together. The swing that they were in was made to accommodate up to three people, and Roger reached over and gave her a hug.

Roger still looked like a bum with a long scraggly beard and hair, baggy Holly overalls, and a ratty straw hat, but to her, he was the friendliest person she had ever met. He didn't judge her, and she wasn't about to judge him.

"Do your parents know where you are this time?" he said after they stopped laughing. "I don't want anything like what happened last time. You know how I feel about lying, and last time you were a little close."

"I did n-not. I t-told the t-truth. I s-said I was at a f-friend's. A-aren't you my f-friend? I said I d-didn't w-want to w-walk home alone, a-and I didn't. W-what part of it w-was a lie?"

"Well, I guess technically you didn't, but there was a little deception. But I guess under the circumstances, I don't think there was an alternative that wouldn't have led to a further unpleasant outcome. What about today?"

"I t-told them I was v-visiting a f-friend after s-school and w-would be a l-little late."

"I guess you left it up to them to guess what friend?"

"You a-are my only f-friend."

"That can't be true. You should have many friends at school."

"I d-don't have any. Y-you and now N-Nanny are the on-only ones I h-have. I d-didn't lie."

"Okay, but I think as much as I insist on my privacy, I think we have to let your parents in on our friendship. I want to meet them and have them over to meet me and see how I live. I don't want to hide anything nor have them feel I am hiding anything. Let's give your mom a call right now, and she can come down so we can have a proper meeting."

"We c-can't. She isn't h-home."

"I thought you said she stayed home while your father took the car to work."

"Mom d-drove Dad to w-work today so sh-she could have the c-car. She h-had some e-errands to run. They d-do that some sometimes. W-when they f-found out I-I was g-going to be at a f- friend's place, th-they'd decided it w-would be a good d-day to do it."

Sending her home was not an option. He could not send her home to be alone. She was too young to be left alone, and if they came home and found her there alone, things would really get bad.

"Well since we have some time together, how about me introducing you to a few new friends?"

He then led her into the barn and through a door into the chicken coop. There were chickens running around in the straw and others sitting on nests in boxlike cubbyholes along the side of the coop.

He then took a basket off a hook on the wall and said, "How about you and I gather some eggs? Just reach in under any of the hens in the box and get the eggs they are sitting on. I'll hold the basket."

"I-I've never seen a r-real live ch-chicken before. Do th-they bite? I'm s-scared."

"They don't bite, they peck. But, no, they won't hurt you. Just reach under them and search for the eggs. Sometimes there won't be any, but other times there could be two or three. It's like an Easter egg hunt. In fact you may find different-colored eggs."

She finally got up enough courage to slowly reach in, and as soon as she did, the chicken looked at her, and she quickly drew her hand back. "I'm s-scared. Sh-she'll b-bite me."

"She won't hurt you. Don't be a chicken."

"Th-that is not f-funny."

But Roger laughed anyway. "Here, let me show you." And he reached in and came out with a green egg. "See, I told you there was nothing to it."

"B-but the egg is g-green. Is it r-rotten?"

"No, this is their natural color. I told you they come in different colors. Different chickens lay different-colored eggs. And they also come in different sizes. That's what makes gathering them so interesting. Now you do it."

"Are th-they green in inside like in the Doc-Dr. Seuss book?"

Roger laughed again. "No, they all are the same inside, but the yokes are a brighter orange than the eggs you buy in the store"

"I h-have seen o-only white eggs b-before. Why a-are the y-yokes from y-your chickens a brighter o-orange than the o-ones in the s-store?"

"Because they are happier. They get to run around and eat all kinds of food that I give them. Now stop stalling and reach in and get an egg."

She finally slowly reached in, then pulled her hand back. Then slowly reached in all the way and pulls out a brown egg which she gently placed in the basket Roger was holding.

"See, that wasn't so scary, was it? That chicken is called a Plymouth Rock. They have feathers that are black-and-white, and they lay brown eggs. The chicken in the next box is my favorite. It is called a Dorking and lays cream-colored eggs. She is very friendly and loves to sit on my lap and talk to me."

"You are m making fun of m me. Chickens c-can't t-talk."

"Why sure they can. They have a language, and if we listen, we can understand them. Just like Nanny when she talks to you. Now check and see if there are any eggs under her."

When she did, she found two eggs. One cream-colored and another that was blue.

"Y-you said she l-laid cr-cream-colored e-eggs. How c-come there is a b-blue one in h-here?"

"The chickens all share the boxes. One chicken will lay an egg and leave. Then another one will come along and lay another in the same box. Oftentimes they prefer to lay eggs in boxes that already have an egg or more, especially if they want to raise a family. Then they adopt all the eggs even if they aren't all their own, which they wouldn't be because most chickens usually only lay two or four eggs a week. That is not enough for a clutch of up to eight chicks as some of them are."

"How d-do you kn-know so much about ch-chickens?"

"If you are going to raise animals, you should know how to take care of them and learn as much about them as you can. Don't you think your mom studied how to raise a child before you were born?"

"But th-that is di-different."

"Is it? Don't you think animals deserve the respect and care we should show to all life? Let's finish gathering the eggs and give them some grain. Then I'll take them in the house, and you can give Nanny a treat and say goodbye before you go home."

As they left the barn, Roger stopped and took some carrots out of a box and handed them to Liza. "Here, go give these to Nanny, and I'll take care of the eggs. She's pretty energetic when it comes to eating, so make sure to let go or she may pull your arm out of its socket. Just give her a hug and say goodbye. I think you should be heading home. We don't want your parents worried about you. And please invite them to come over this evening so we can meet. I'll try to dress up a little and be presentable. Don't use the front door. It is always locked, and I never use it. Just have them drive around to the back porch where the car can't be seen from the street."

Liza fed Nanny the carrots and said her goodbyes, then met Roger on the porch. They gave each other a big hug, and he said, "Now hurry along home, I'll see you later. And another thing, when you get home, run to your mother, give her a big hug, and tell her you love her. When your dad comes home, do the same to him."

At that he tipped his straw hat and bowed and said, "Until next time, princess."

As she skipped down the driveway, she giggled a little.

Chapter 5

The Petersons

When Liza arrived home, her mother was in the kitchen, preparing dinner. Liza ran to her, gave her a big hug, and said, "I l love you, Mama."

Her mother looked down at her, a little shocked and her mouth open. "What has got into you? You must have had a good day at your new friend's."

"Mom w-what is a sa-sanitation en-engineer? My f-friend says th-that is w-what Daddy is. A-and that it is a-a very im-important job. It's l-like your job. Y-you keep the h-house clean and-and he k-keeps the city c-clean. And th-they are b-both very im-important. I sh-should be v-very proud of b-both of you."

Jean, her mother stopped stirring the soup she was preparing and turned to Liza. "Who is this new friend of yours? This does not sound like the language a little girl your age would be using. She must be something special."

When her father, Scott, came home, she gave him the same greeting. As Liza hugged him, he gave his wife a questioning look. She just gave him a shrug of the shoulders.

When Liza went to her room and told them to call her when supper was ready, Jean just said, "She has been like that since she came home a half hour ago. She also has repeated comments that her new friend said that is quite peculiar. Such as asking me what a sanitation engineer was. Her friend says that is what you are."

"She is right, but that doesn't sound like what two little girls would be talking about or even aware of what the word means. She is either very smart or very strange. But I can't complain about the change in attitude she has shown."

"Hopefully, at supper we will get a little more information about her new friend," Liza's mother said. "Now get cleaned up and take a shower. You stink. Supper will be ready in a half hour."

"Yes, dear. You wouldn't smell too good either if you worked all day as a sanitation engineer."

"Get out of here."

Then they both laughed.

When they all sat down to supper, they tried to coax more information out of Liza about her friend, but she was not forthcoming and had to be careful to not give any indication that her new friend was a man. However, she had to keep her promise not to lie.

Finally she said, "My f-friend wants to m-meet you and said th-that tonight w-would be a g-good time. I'm n-not supposed to-to visit a- again un-until you can m-meet. I p-promised. P-please."

"What do you think, Scott? I respect parents that want to meet the parents of their child's friend."

"I agree. I'm anxious to meet this family. Besides, we really haven't developed any friendships since moving here. Maybe it is about time. Liza, what time do they want us over there?"

Liza was giddy with joy, but she was a little apprehensive. "A-anytime y-you are ready. But it sh-should be before d-dark."

"I think that is a good idea. I'll clean up. Liza, will you help with the dishes? We'll just put them in the sink with water, and I will wash them when we get back. It will be dark in another hour."

Since they all had finished their meal, Scott offered to help clear the table, and soon they were all in the car. They were anxious for Liza to foster relationships in this new town since encounters in previous homes and towns were less than pleasant and eventually led to their moving here. It was a move of a last resort and a big leap. They had spent everything they had to make the move, selling everything possible and driving an old vehicle thousands of miles to find a community they thought would accept their daughter.

But the move was not entirely due to their interest in providing a better environment for their daughter. Scott's parents were killed in a car accident when he was only six. His grandmother, who was not in good health herself, took over his care. Her husband had died before Scott was born, so she was the only relative he had left. Scott worked at whatever he could to help pay expenses, and with government help, they just got by. When he met Jean and they were married, the three of them lived together. With two incomes and his grandmother's social security, their standard of living got better. However, four years later, a year after Liza was born, his grandmother's health deteriorated to the point where they had to put her in a rest home.

Jean was an orphan. Her mother was an addict, and when she was placed in jail, Jean became the ward of the state and was passed from foster home to foster home from the time she was five. Her mother never got off drugs and died soon after. They never found out the identity of Jean's father. With their marriage, they felt they could have something they both longed for—a family. But tragedy hit again. The difficult birth of Liza left Jean unable to have any more children. A major blow because they were both looking forward to three or four children. Now Liza became the center of their life.

Scott's grandmother died two years after being placed in the rest home, but the expenses her stay incurred left them in financial debt. They worked hard to get out of debt and managed to, but it left them with a low-income apartment and no savings to speak of. Liza by now was in grade school, and again they were faced with another challenge. Because of her stuttering, other students teased her to the point that she came home crying every day. Her emotional challenges affected her learning. Soon they moved to try to find another environment. But it didn't work. They knew they needed to make a more dramatic change, and they hoped Alderwood would be the answer.

Living expenses would be lower, and since their funds were very limited, they took a chance. They were surprised when the local bank qualified them for a loan on the house and took it as a sign that things were looking up. Now this was another positive sign. Not having any known relatives on either side left Liza completely alone. Having a friend here could made a big difference, and they didn't want to take a chance of messing it up.

As they followed Liza's directions, they found out it was only a couple of blocks away, and when she told her father to turn up the dirt driveway, there were some questions. Although almost completely hidden by weeds and overgrown rose bushes, they noticed a sign that read "Private Property, Keep Out." The sign had been placed there when the property was vacant to discourage visitors and vandalism, and Roger never bothered to remove it.

"Are you sure this is the right place?" her mother remarked. I have heard rumors about this property, and they were not good."

"It is all-all right, it is not h-haunted. M-my friends live h-here." "Friends?" Her father said as he drove up the driveway. "I thought you said a friend. How many friends do you have here?" "Well, s-several, but r-really only t-two."

"Now things are getting stranger and stranger," he said as he stopped the car at the top of the driveway and saw an old man standing by a porch. Liza opened the car door and ran over to Roger and gave him a big hug. He was dressed in a clean and neat dress shirt and clean jeans that didn't have any holes or patches. His beard and hair had been washed, trimmed, and combed neatly. And he did not have on his ragged old straw hat. Overall, he looked rather respectable.

Her mother was a little taken aback and stayed in the car. Scott got out and walked over to Liza and Roger and said, "What is going on here?"

"This is my f-friend, Daddy. His n-name is R-Roger."

Scott was not sure what to say now or how to react. But he finally said, "Liza, get back in the car."

"No, he is my f-friend."

Roger, recognizing the situation, stepped in. "Mr. Peterson, I know this is a shock and may seem unorthodox, and I assure you, so do I. However, I assure you my relationship with your daughter poses no threat. Our meeting was totally unexpected and unplanned. I wanted to call you immediately upon our meeting, but she adamantly convinced me not to. I respected her wishes but insisted that you come and meet me before I would allow her to visit my place again. Believe me, I would no longer harm your daughter or cause her any unpleasantness no more than you would. I told her she had loving parents and it would be up to them if she could visit here again."

"She did give us a hug and told us she loved us when we met her at home. Did you have something to do with that?"

"Yes, D-Daddy, he did."

"She is a very lovely and smart young lady. I respect her wishes, but you are her parents. It is up to her, not me, to tell you what she feels and what she wants and then it's up to you to decide what you feel is best for her."

"Yes, Daddy, h-he told me to, and he-he said you h-had a very im- important job. He s-said I should re-respect your job and y-you. He w-would never h-harm me. He p-protects me."

Her mother now stepped out of the car. "What do you mean by 'he protects' you?"

"I d-don't want to m-move again, I l like it here," she said with tears in her eyes.

"Oh, honey," Jean said. "We're not going to move. What made you think that?"

"We m-moved before be-because of h-how children m-made fun of me. We m-moved here f-for the s-same reason. I don't w-want to m- move again. Roger w-will take c-care of me," she said with tears in her eyes.

Her mother got out of the car. "We are so sorry. We didn't know you knew. We tried to keep it from you. But we also moved so your father could get a better job. But what do you mean Roger will protect you?"

Then Roger and Liza narrated the events of the day of the meeting.

Scott finally spoke up. "I guess I should thank you. I may have misjudged you. But who is this other person she says is a friend?"

Liza grabbed his hand and dragged him toward the coral. "C-come on, Daddy, you can m-meet her."

And there was Nanny at the coral fence with her "na na na." "See, sh-she is s-saying hello." Her parents laughed.

As she opened the gate, her mother yelled, "Liza, don't go in there. You could get hurt."

Liza ignored her and continued on in, where Nanny was waiting for her. Liza gave her a big hug, and Nanny responded with a "na na" and gave her a little nudge with her head.

"See, she j-just wants to p-play. She w-wouldn't hurt me. She is my f-friend."

Her parents just laughed again and smiled as they saw their daughter laughing and having fun for the first time in years. Roger had receded to his swing on the porch to watch. It made him feel good to see Liza having fun and her parents happy as well. Scott and Jean soon joined Roger on the porch.

"I have never seen her so happy," commented Jean.

"Yes," Roger said. "They make a good pair. They wear me out just watching them."

"She came home crying almost every day where we used to live due to the teasing she endured because of her stuttering. We had hoped it could possibly be different here. When she came home with dry eyes, we felt it would be all right. Unbeknownst to us, she did know the reason for the moves. It seems you have been instrumental in her alleviating the same situation here."

"I only gave her an opportunity. She made the choice to face it head-on. It doesn't hurt, however, that she now is the only one walking home on this side of the street. She now holds her head high because she has a higher sense of self-esteem. That is something that is helped by having a friend who loves you unconditionally. Nanny needed a friend, and her love is unconditional."

Scott said, "By the way, I never caught your name," and he extended his hand for a shake.

"Well, I suppose you can't catch what I don't throw your way. I go by Roger, just Roger."

"Glad to meet you, Roger. My name is Scott Peterson, and this is my wife Jean. It appears you already have met our daughter Liza." And they shook hands.

Jean, who had been intent on watching her daughter, cut in, "This is such a sudden change in her attitude. I have never seen her so happy. I have no doubt she has made two friends here. I can't argue with anything that makes my little girl so happy. And there is no doubt you and this place has a lot to do with it. I can see your friendship is also unconditional. I think we have all found a new friend." And with that, she reached over and shook his hand as her husband had.

Just then Liza called, "Mom, Dad, c-come and m-meet Nanny. She w-won't hurt you."

"It is getting late and beginning to get chilly. Maybe we all better go inside," her mother said.

Liza finally gave Nanny a big hug and said goodbye and joined them on the porch. "We c-can't go inside."

"But why not?" her mother said.

"Mrs. Peterson, she is right. I made it clear to her when she first came here I do not allow others inside my house. I have a problem with privacy. Allowing Liza, or any other child, alone in my house would not be proper and would make me very uncomfortable. How it would look to others would be even worse. I don't feel comfortable allowing anyone inside at this point. It is, as I said, a personal issue of privacy and not a reflection on anyone else."

"It is getting a little chilly out and starting to get dark. I think we ought to be getting home. We can come back another day and get to know each other better," Scott said.

"Before you go," Roger said, "I have something for you. Just a minute, I'll be right back."

He then went into the house and came out with a basket covered with a towel. "I'm afraid I don't have any need for these. I'll let Liza explain when you get home. You can return the basket whenever you get a chance. There is no hurry."

Liza took the basket and smiled. When her mother questioned her further, Liza could not keep it a secret. "These are E-Easter eggs."

"An Easter egg is one that has been colored. I thought Roger didn't let anyone in his house. Did you color them out here?"

"But th-these are m-magic eggs. They c-come out colored." Roger and Liza just looked at each other and gave a wink. "I helped g- gather them."

"Liza, I hope you were careful. Chickens could bite you."

"Mama, c-chickens do not b-bite. They peck. And I kn-know a lot a- about c-chickens! Roger t-taught me. He kn-knows everything a- about them. He t-taught me."

Scott had already gotten in the car and was waiting. "Come on, get in, we can discuss wildlife habits when we get home. Nice to meet you. We'll talk and get to know each other later."

Liza let Roger give her a hug. As she was holding the eggs, she could only lean against him, and he said, "Goodbye, princess. I'll take care of your kingdom while you are gone."

She just smiled and gave a little giggle.

By then, Jean was in the car and she said goodbye and gave Roger a wave as they drove down the driveway.

"What was that he called you, Liza?" her father asked.

"He c-calls me a p-princess, and-and his place is my k-kingdom. I'm not a r-real p-princess. H-he just c-calls me that."

"Well, I agree with him. I think you are a princess."

With the eggs in her lap, Liza rode home with a big smile on her face. It had been a good day, and she was happy.

When they got in the house, Jean said, "Give me the eggs, and I'll put them in the refrigerator. When she lifted the towel and saw the eggs, she remarked, "These eggs are all different colors."

"I t-told you they w-were E-Easter eggs." Then she started pointing to individual ones. "That c-cream-colored one c-comes from a D-Dorking. And th-that b-blue one an Araucana. S-sometimes they lay g-green eggs. The w-white egg c-comes from a S-Silkie. She is f- funny looking w-with puffy cheeks. Those p-pink ones come f-from a barred Rock. She is b-black-and-w-white chicken, and the p-prettiest one. But Roger's f-favorite is the D-Dorking because sh-she is very f- friendly and sits on h-his lap and t-talks to him."

Her father could not hold it in any longer and burst out laughing. "A dorky chicken that talks to you. Now I have heard of everything."

Liza yelled back, "It is Dorking, not d-dorky. And R-Roger says sh- she t-talks to him l-like N-Nanny t-talks to me."

But Scott was out of control. "Now we have a talking goat."

Jean now felt she had to step in. "Now stop it, Scott, she is serious." But she couldn't hold it in any longer and began to laugh as well.

By now Liza stomped on the floor and screamed, "But it's t true. They do t-talk in their own l-language. We just h-have to learn to l-listen." And she began to cry.

"I'm sorry," he father said. "I believe you. It just sounds funny, and I couldn't help myself. But I can see you have learned a lot about eggs and chickens. Tell us about the other eggs."

"I d-don't remember the r-rest, but Roger s-says he will t-teach me more. He kn-knows a lot about a-animals and nature," she said through sniffles.

"Maybe he can teach us all about animals and nature. He seems to be a very smart person. Now it is getting a little late, and you have school tomorrow, so go get cleaned up and get your pajamas on and get ready for bed."

"All right, b-but it's true." Then she hugged each of her parents, said "I love you," and ran off to her room.

After Liza was out of earshot, Scott said to his wife, "You know I don't remember a more enjoyable evening. Even though at one point it looked like it could be a bad situation. It shows it's not fair to prejudge. I love you, Jean." And he gave her a hug.

"Did Roger tell you to say that?"

Then they both had another good laugh.

Chapter 6

Getting to Know Each Other

That Friday, Jean told Liza to meet her at Roger's after school. She planned to go there to get to know Roger better. She wanted to talk to him alone before Liza arrived. When she got there, he was out working in the garden, and Nanny was bleating. She walked toward Roger. His back was toward her. But before she even got close, and without turning around, he said, "Good afternoon, Jean, to what do I owe the honor of this visit?"

"How did you know someone was here, and how did you know it was me? I was quiet and not close enough for you to possibly hear me."

"Nanny told me you were here."

"Liza told us she talks to you, but we laughed at her. I guess we were wrong. But how did you know it was me?"

"Oh, animals do talk. We just have to learn their language and listen."

"But all she says is 'ba ba ba.'"

"If it were Liza, it would have been louder and more repetitious. If a stranger, it would have been long and drawn out. She knows you, so she had a calm, steady greeting. Since you are the only ones that have come here that she has met, it had to be you."

She was taken aback when he turned around. Unlike his dress of their first meeting, he now wore old Holly coveralls, a dirty old torn shirt, and the ragged straw hat that he wore when he and Liza first met. "I'm beginning to believe you do talk to the animals."

"I'm sure you didn't come here to discuss my relationships with my animals. But since, as you can see, I am engaged in weeding, maybe you would like to join me as we talk?"

"I brought your basket back, and I just came to talk and get to know each other, but I guess I could assist since I see you are busy. I'm not a farmer, but I'll give it a try. What do you want me to do? By the way, I asked Liza to meet me here after school."

"Just wait here, and I'll get you another hoe and a pair of gloves." At that he walked to his storage shed and brought back a hoe and pair of gloves. "Put these on. They may be a little big, but they will do. We are taking out the weeds between the potatoes. The potatoes are the plants on the raised ground on each side of the row, while anything in between are weeds that have to be removed. Now watch as I demonstrate. I'll do this row, and you do the one next to me." And he proceeded to dig out the weeds. She tried to imitate him. See, you got it. Now what do you want to talk about?"

"I just wanted to get to know you better and give you some information about us. To start with, what is your last name, and where did you live before you came here? Since my daughter is determined to spend time here, I feel it essential we know each other better." In the meantime, she had stopped weeding and was leaning on her hoe.

"You missed a few there," Roger said.

"I guess I'm not a very good farmer."

"We aren't farming. We are gardening. But I guess it is time for a break. Here, give me your gloves and hoe, and I'll meet you on the porch." At that he took her hoe and gloves, took them to the shed with his own, and then met her on the porch.

Once they were relaxed in the swing on the porch, he began his introduction. "I'll try to make it easy for you. I don't use a last name. I am a simple person. I live a simple life, trying to be as independent and private as possible. I raise my own chickens for the eggs. I have a goat for milk that I use to make butter and cheese when possible. I have bees for honey. I have fruit trees and a garden of which I preserve as much as possible. I grind my own wheat for flour. I bake and cook almost everything I consume. The only items I purchase from the stores are staples such as salt, yeast, and other spices. At times I buy sugar but usually use honey in its place. As far as my past, I have never been arrested or committed anything close to a crime. Although I am adamantly against violence, I have served in two wars. I feel the word 'hate' should be left totally out of our minds and language. I believe in a complete tolerance of others' ideas and totally against discrimination of any kind. I have never been in debt and believe in hard work and honesty at all times. Any form of cheating or taking advantage of others is an abomination to me. Lying, as you know, is another pet peeve and am totally against it. We should be tolerant of others and treat them with respect and love. However, although I am not running from my past, it is not an open topic. My concern is the present and the future. Have I answered most of your questions?"

"I don't remember asking a question. But I guess so. You have been pretty thorough."

"Excuse me a minute," he said as he got up and went into the house.

She sat nervously for about ten minutes. When he came back, he emerged with a plate of cookies, bread with honey, butter and jam, and a small pitcher of milk with a couple of glasses.

"You didn't have to go to the trouble of furnishing refreshments," she commented.

"I wouldn't be a good host if I didn't. Besides, it is no trouble, and everything is made or raised on the property."

"You mentioned being self-sufficient, but I never believed to what extent. I don't believe it."

"What don't you believe?"

"That you can provide all this and that you have time to do everything. How do you manage it all?"

"It's just a matter working with nature. There is a time for everything. You don't have to do everything at the same time, or even the same season. You do what you can when it needs to be done, and don't worry about things out of your control."

Then she took a sip of the milk. "Are you sure this milk isn't sour?"

"That is the same response Liza had when she first drank it. It's Nanny's milk. I guess you haven't had goat's milk before. You'll get used to it. It is actually better for you than cow's milk. She doesn't produce a lot, but it is enough for me and enough to make butter and, at times, cheese. I used the honey from my bees, eggs from my chickens, Nanny's milk, and wheat I ground to make the cookies and bread. No additives or preservatives. I hope you like them."

As she tried the cookies and bread with jam, she said, "Hmm, these are wonderful, and I guess I'll get used to the milk. I don't believe you did all this."

"I'm glad you enjoy them. It is nice to see someone enjoy things. After all, making others' lives more enjoyable should be the goal of all of us. And it makes me happy seeing others happy."

At that they sat, enjoying the snacks and taking in the beautiful day and at times engaging in small talk.

Chapter 7

Gifts and Decisions

In a short time, Liza arrived. She rushed to her mother and gave her a big hug and told her she loved her.

"I love you too, sweetheart," her mother replied.

Then she put her books down, gave Roger a hug, grabbed a cookie, and ran for the coral. She immediately opened the gate where Nanny was bleating and anxiously waiting for her. Within a minutes of play, she called, "C-come on, M-Mama. Come a-and meet N-Nanny. She w-wants to p-play with you."

Roger stood up and took Jean's hand and said, "Shall we join them? We shouldn't let them have all the fun."

Jean then stood up and walked with him to the pen. But when Roger opened the gate, she hesitated.

Liza walked over to her with Nanny on her hip, and said, "It's okay, N-Nanny won't h-hurt you. She j-just wants to p-play. Pet her a-and she w-will be your f-friend for l-life."

Jean hesitantly reached out and petted Nanny on the nose. "She is so soft, it feels good."

"See, Mama, s-she can be y-your friend too. I l love her."

"Well," Roger finally spoke up. "I guess she has a new owner if you want."

"You mean y-you w-would give her to me?" Liza said.

"She is not mine to give. She gave herself to you. You just have to accept her offer as long as your parents approve. However, I believe it best she stay here."

"Mama, c-can I, c-can I?"

Jean stood there in shock but finally answered, "If your father says it's okay, I guess. It is like Roger said, she gave herself to you. I don't think I can question her. I don't understand goat talk like Roger." Then they all laughed. "But she has to stay here."

Liza ran to her mother and gave her a big hug and then gave Roger one. Nanny, right by her side, gave Jean a little butt, apparently showing her approval. And when Jean gave a little "oh" in surprise, they all laughed again.

When Nanny turned and ran, Liza said, "She ta-tagged you, n-now you h-have to tag her."

Roger said, "Go ahead, it's time you learned the game."

She took off after Nanny while Roger and Liza stood back and laughed. Of course, Jean could never catch Nanny and soon stumbled over to Roger and said, "I am too old for this, but it feels good to pretend to be a child again, especially with my daughter and her friend."

"Come on," Roger said. "Let's go back to the porch and leave the two to play. There may be something I can do to help."

On the way back to the porch, Jean asked, "What do you mean?"

"We still have a problem, as you have brought out, concerning Liza's academics and speech problem. I think I may be able to help, or at least try. I know she's smart, but I believe it is her lack of self-esteem and ability to concentrate that is holding her back. Just being around other students that have caused her discomfort prevents her from concentrating and paying attention in school. I don't claim to be a teacher or psychologist, but I think I would like to try something. I do have a college degree and have done some counseling while there. I also minored in psychology and did research in and wrote a paper on stuttering. There are no guarantees, but I would like to try. She could stop by after school two or three times a week, and we could spend a couple of hours together. If you are interested, you could talk it over with your husband and let me know."

"You would do that?"

"There is nothing important than a child's mind and their happiness. You have been through a lot. It is time you got a break, and if there is anything I can do, I would deem it a privilege. You would be in complete control, and I would keep you up-to-date on any developments. You don't have to decide now. I want you to go home and discuss it with your husband first and let me know. Now it is getting late, and I'm sure you have things to get ready for supper, and Liza, I'm sure, has homework. Go home, take care of your family. I'll talk to you later."

At that she said, "Thank you for everything. Liza has never had a pet before. Wait until she tells her dad she now owns a goat. I can't wait to see his face."

She then called Liza and told her it was time to go home.

Reluctantly, she gave Nanny a hug and said goodbye. She then ran to Roger, gave him a big hug, and said, "Thank you. I l love you."

"I love you too, princess," he said. But to hide the tears in his eyes, he turned and walked to the house.

"Come on," her mother said. "Your father will be home soon, and we have to get supper ready." And they departed down the driveway with Liza skipping all the way.

When Scott got home, and after Liza's greeting, he confronted his wife, "Well, how did things go today? Liza seems to be in an exceptionally good mood."

"I think you better sit down."

"Is it that bad?"

"Not really bad, just unexpected. First, Liza has a new pet."

At that Scott stood up and said in a loud voice, "What!"

"Keep your voice down, Liza will hear you, and settle down. She won't bring the pet here. In fact, you have already met it."

"What are you talking about?"

"Roger has given Nanny to Liza, or, as Roger said, Nanny gave herself to Liza. She will remain where she is, and Roger will take complete responsibility and care of her. But it is something she can call her own. He feels it will help in her self-esteem and attitude. But I have bigger news."

"What could be bigger than getting a goat as a pet?"

"Roger has agreed to tutor Liza after school. He has a college degree and has studied psychology and done research in the field of stuttering. He has also been a counselor while in college. He says he can't guarantee anything but is willing to try. We could set they days, and he would report progress. He says it is up to us, and without our permission and support, he will not do it. He is determined to help Liza in any way he can, but only with our go-ahead. Scott, think, it would give me the opportunity to find a job and work at least part-time. We can't go on much longer without additional income. We were fortunate to get the loan on this house, but you know as well as I we can't keep up the payments without additional income."

"You know how I feel about you going to work. Liza needs you to be here."

"But can't you see this situation with Roger would allow me time for at least a part-time job? And he said we can set the days and hours. He says his time is completely open, which he could work with a schedule that works for me. I don't see any negatives. I spent time with him today, and I believe him to be completely trustworthy. He is totally invested in the well-being of our daughter."

"This is a lot to take in all at once. But I have to be realistic. You are right about our finances. For the life of me, I don't understand why the mortgage was approved. We knew we couldn't continue the payments unless I got a raise or we had some other source. I guess we were both just being optimistic. We were desperate, and we jumped into something that was too good to be true. Now I guess you are right. We have no choice. Your taking on a part-time job would help out, at least for now. So even though I don't like it, I agree to support you and the situation with Roger, as I see it would be the only way it could work. So I guess we have a tutor, or babysitter, and I have a working wife."

"Thank you, honey. I know things will work out. I feel it in my bones."

"Then get your bones over here and give me a big hug and a kiss," he said as he stood up from the chair he was sitting on.

Chapter 8

Lessons Begin

Three days later, on a Wednesday, it was decided Liza would stop by Roger's after school with her homework. He had brought out the only two chairs he had and set them up at the small table on the porch for a makeshift desk. Relaxed on the swing was no way to become serious while trying to take homework seriously.

When Liza came near the top of the driveway, she began to run to Nanny's pen. But Roger stepped out in front of her. At first she did not recognize him. He had no hat on but had the attire of a clean and almost church-appropriate shirt and pants and dress shoes on. It was completely out of character for him. He stood with his arms folded over his chest. "Where do you think you are going, young lady?" he said.

Liza just stood there in shock, not knowing what to do or say.

"Not yet, you haven't earned a recess yet. First we have some work to do." Then he gave her a big smile and said, "Now give me a big hug." And he went to her and gave her a bear hug.

This was not what Liza was expecting. She was confused. What happened to her old friend? She did not return the same smile. "Now is that the picture of a princess? A princess holds her head high and always has a smile on her face."

Liza replied, "But I a am not a real p-princess."

"You are to me, and while you are here, you will be one, and a princess has to be well educated. Now stand up straight, put your shoulders back, and give me a big smile. It is time for this princess to begin her education."

Liza's parents told her to stop by Roger's after school. That he was going to assist her in her schoolwork, but she was not prepared for this. With his arms still around her, he led her to the makeshift desk on the porch and sat her down in one chair as he took his place on the other. "Now what subject do we have today that you are struggling with?"

She laid down her school books and handed him her math book. "I don't un-understand figures an-and don't see w-why I h-have to l-learn them."

"Come with me," he said and stood up, taking her hand. He led her to the barn.

"Are we g-going to g-gather eggs? I like g-gathering eggs."

When they got to the chicken enclosure, he told her to count the number of chickens. "Don't y-you know how m-many you have?" she asked.

"I know how many there are. But I want you to count them for me."

So she started to count them. When she finished, she told him there were twelve. He then asked her to count the ones in the nesting boxes. She counted and said six.

"Twelve chickens, and what does twelve equal?"

"I do not u-understand, t-twelve is t-twelve."

"When your mother goes to the store and buys eggs, how many does she says she has to get?"

"She says she n-needs a d-dozen."

"And how many are in a dozen?"

"They c-come in a c-carton, I d-don't know."

"This is going to be harder than I thought. Now you counted twelve chickens. Twelve is a dozen. So how many chickens do I have in words other than twelve?"

She thought for a while, then said, "A d-dozen?" But it was in the form of a question.

"Now how many chickens were in their nesting boxes?"

"Six."

"And six is what part or fraction of twelve?"

"I don't kn-know. I don't un-understand fr-fractions."

"Sure you do, you just don't think you do. I am going to help you out. A dozen is twelve, right? So if six is half of twelve, what part of a dozen is six?"

Liza thought a little, looked at Roger inquisitively for a while, then finally answered, "Half?" But it was again in the form of a question.

Roger gave her a big hug and smiled and led her back to the porch. "This is not going to be easy. I think we better start from scratch."

She was in fourth grade and by now should be studying fractions. When they said she was struggling, it was no exaggeration. For an hour and a half, they worked with pencil and paper. He drew pictures and made games of things. She finally showed signs of some understanding but had a ways to go. He then told her she could go play with Nanny while he came up with some ideas for their next lesson.

Jean showed up to walk Liza home as he was formulating a new pedagogy. Liza waved to her mother as Jean joined Roger on the porch.

"How are things going?" Jean asked.

Roger replied, "I know she is smart, but we have an uphill battle ahead of us, especially when it comes to math."

Liza had closed the coral and was now headed to the porch to join her mother and Roger.

"I think it's better we discuss this sometime later. Liza is about to join us, and the topic should be kept from young ears."

Jean took the hint and turned to greet her daughter with a smile and a hug.

Roger then turned to Liza and said, "Shall we show your mom how we gather eggs?"

Liza's eyes lit up as she grabbed her mom's hand and dragged her to the barn.

"Hurry up, M-mom. I-It's lots of f-fun."

By the time they were finished, they had ten eggs. And Liza was smiling and held the basket up to her mom. "See, th-they are E- Easter eggs. Isn't it f-fun, like going o-on a Easter e-egg hunt."

Roger and Jean both laughed, and Roger said, "Would you like to take them home?"

"Can we, Mom? I like E-Easter eggs. Th-they are so p-pretty."

"Of course, as long as Roger says we can. That way I can cross eggs off our shopping list. Now I think we better be getting home and start supper for your father."

After hugs and thank-yous were exchanged all around, Liza and her mother turned and waved as they walked down the driveway to go home. On the way home, Jean mentioned to Liza she wanted to find a job to help with expenses. They were struggling despite that Scott was working hard. His job did not pay that well, and he was at entry-level pay. He volunteered to do overtime, but the job seldom required it. Jean asked if she would like to visit Roger's place a few days a week while she worked. Liza jumped at the idea, and they continued home with Liza skipping along with a smile. Her mother took the basket of eggs from her, afraid she would break them.

When Scott arrived home and received a hug and "I love you" from Liza, and Liza had retired to her room, Jean discussed the issue of taking a job with him. She explained the agreement with Roger. Despite his reservations, he knew their financial situation was desperate, and he finally agreed to try it. But first he wanted to talk to Roger personally, so he told Jean he would go there after supper.

After supper, he told Liza he had an errand to run and would be back in about an hour. Jean knew what he was talking about, but Liza asked if she could go with him. He told her it was something he had to take care of alone.

When he got to Roger's, Roger was in the house, so he knocked on the door. He asked if it would be all right if they could come inside and talk. Roger said, "We can sit on the porch. I am not comfortable, as I said, with people in my house. I assume this has to do with the arrangement I made with your wife. I'm glad you came over. You are the head of the house, and I would have no other way than to make sure you were completely on board with everything."

"I don't approve of her working, but the added income would come in handy. I appreciate your desire to help out, and Jean says you feel confident you can help Liza in her school studies and possibly help with the stuttering problem."

"Nothing is more important than the well-being of a child's mental attitude and happiness. That includes their attitude towards themselves. Your family has been dealt a raw deal in life. Liza has especially been affected, to no fault of her own, or yours. I know how much you love her and would do anything for her. I would like to help if I can. Together I think we can make a difference. I am willing to try, and, as I told your wife, I do have a little training that may help. I know you have done everything you could, and moving here was an effort to do so. But sometimes no matter what we do, sometimes outside help can make a difference. Believe me, I will make sure she is safe and properly taken care of here. Now that I have presented my side, what would you like to ask or say?"

"Jean was right. You seem to cover everything pretty well before we ask the questions. I think you covered most of the areas I came to discuss. What days would you be available, and how long would you be available?"

"I am here twenty-four hours a day seven days a week. You tell me what schedule would be best for you. You can pick her up at your convenience. I would not like her walking home along. You can pick the days she visits. As I said, you will be in complete control."

"I don't know what to say. It will ease things financially, and from what I have seen, Liza loves it here. Thank you."

"No need to thank me. She is a ray of sunshine to this place. But I must warn you, she is going to work. We will be doing homework and going over assignments as I try to work on her speech issue. We need to build her self-esteem first in order for her to open up and want to learn and improve."

They then shook hands, and Scott again said "thank you," and he got in his car and drove away.

When he got home, Jean met him at the door. "Well, how did it go?"

"I guess you can start looking for a job. I don't like you working, but we know without the extra income, what little savings we have will be gone soon, and we would not be able to make the mortgage. This may be the opportunity we have been praying for."

She gave him a big hug. "I think it is. I feel good about it and, for the first time in years, am sure everything will be all right."

Chapter 9

Teaching in Earnest

Three days later, on a Wednesday, it was decided Liza would stop by Roger's after school with her homework. He had brought out the only two chairs he had and set them up at the makeshift desk—his small table on the back porch. He did not feel relaxed on the swing because it was not conducive for learning. He had to set up an environment as close to a school setting as possible. There would be time later for getting an education in life. But today was to be devoted to a more academic education.

When Liza came close to the top of the driveway, she began to run to Nanny's pen, but out stepped someone in formal attire to block her path. Instead of her old friend in shabby, dirty clothes and straw hat, out stepped the person who met with her parents a week ago. He stood with his arms folded over his chest and a stern look on his face. "Not yet, you haven't earned a recess." As he put a smile on his face, he said, "Now come here and give me a hug," and he reached out with his arms wide.

This was not what Liza was expecting. She was confused. What happened to her old friend? She finally walked up to him with her head down to give him the requested hug. But the usual smile was missing. "Now is that the picture of a princess? A princess holds her head high and always has a smile on her face, especially for her subjects."

"But I am n-not a real p-princess."

"You are to me and this property, and while you are here, I would like you to act like one. Now stand up straight, put your shoulders back, and give me a big smile." Her parents instructed her to pay attention and do what he told her to, so she did as instructed. He then again put his arms around her and led her to the impromptu desk he had set up on the porch. "Remember, head up, shoulders back. You are a proud princess. And a princess has to be educated, and I understand education is not your cup of tea."

"I don't l-like s-school, it is s-stupid."

"We all need to receive an education. Some more than others, and formal education is essential for us to cope with the life in this day and age. Now what subject are you struggling with today?"

She then pulls out her books and points to the math book. "I do n not understand f-fractions or mul-multiplications and do not see w-why I need to l-learn them."

"Come with me." Roger took her by the hand, and they headed to the barn. When inside, they went into the pen where the chickens were, and he asked her to count the chickens. They were all penned up inside, so all were inside, either on the floor of straw or in the laying boxes.

"You h-had me c-count them S-Saturday," she replied.

"I know, but this is a review. Now count the chickens, please."

She then counted them and answered, "Twelve."

"Good, now how many are in the laying boxes?"

Again she counted and answered, "Six."

"And what is another word that means twelve?"

"I don't un-understand what y-you mean."

"When your mother goes to the store, does she say I need twelve eggs?"

"No, sh-she says we n-need a -dozen eggs."

"So how many eggs are there in a dozen? I'm sure you counted how many were in a carton, didn't you?"

"Twelve?" she finally said, more in the form of a question.

"So a dozen is another term for twelve. Now you counted six in the boxes. What part of twelve, or a dozen, using fractions, is that?"

She had to think for a while, so he stepped in to help out. "If I cut an apple in equal portions and give you an equal part, how much do you have?"

"I would h-have a h-half."

"So if I have a dozen chickens and six are in the nesting boxes, what part of my chickens out of the twelve, a dozen, are in boxes?"

"One-h-half," she finally says after thinking awhile. But again it was more of a question.

Roger realized this was not going to be easy. Liza's math skills were far behind where they should be at this point. They were going to have to go back to basics, and he believed an unorthodox method may be called for. But he forged on. "How many chickens do you count that are white?"

"Three." This time she was a little excited.

"And, in fractions, what part of the dozen chickens do those three make up?"

"I don't k-know."

So he pulled some change out of his pocket he had put there in anticipation of being a possible learning tool.

He put one of the coins in her hand.

"What is that?"

"It is a q-quarter," she said with a question on her face.

"And why is it called a quarter?"

"I don't kn-know, it just is."

"It is called a quarter because it takes four to equal one dollar. In fractions, that is one-fourth. So if I have twelve chickens and six equals one half and three equals half of six, you have one quarter. So if the three chickens make up one quarter of the chickens, what is another word for one quarter? A quarter is what part of one dollar?"

"One-fourth?" she says again as a question.

"That's right, but don't question yourself. Just think it out and answer with confidence. Now let's go back to the porch, and we can work things out on paper." He went into the house and, in a few minutes, came back with some chalk and paper. "Here is a brown piece of chalk. I want you to draw and color six chickens on your paper."

At the same time, he took out pieces of white and black chalk and drew and colored three chickens of each color. He then pulled out an apple from his pocket and cut it in half and handed her one-half. "Now what part of the apple do you have?'

"I have a h-half."

"And that is a fraction. And means it takes two parts to make a whole. Remember the coins? How many quarters does it take to make a whole dollar?"

"Four," she replied.

"So a quarter is another fraction that stands for one-fourth. So we use fractions all the time. So now let's build on this base. A fraction is a portion of a whole. One-fourth is a quarter of one. One-third means it takes three parts to make one, and one-fifth means it takes five parts to make a whole, and so on. So how many dimes does it take to make a whole?"

"Ten, it t-takes ten dimes to m-make a whole d-dollar."

"Now you're getting it. You drew six brown chickens on your paper.

What fraction is that of the whole of twelve that I have?"

"Six is h-half of twelve. So it is half."

"Now how many chickens have I drawn on my paper?" And he showed her his drawings.

"Your ch-chickens look f-funny," she remarked as she giggled a little.

"I never claimed to be an artist. Now how many chickens do I have?"

"You have s-six."

"So I have half, the same as you. Now how many are white, and what fraction are they of the whole, which is twelve?"

She thought a little then answered, "They are a q-quarter or one-fourth."

"Are you sure?"

"Yes."

"Now that's the way you answer things—with confidence. There is one other thing we need to work on today before taking a break." And he took out six forks out of his pocket. "I want you to count these forks."

As he put them down one at a time, he said, "Now count them as I put them down on the table, and say fork as you count them."

As he put the first one down she said, "One f-fork."

"That's wrong, let's start again."

"That is n-not wrong, th-there is one f-fork," she said adamantly.

"Yes, there is one fork, but I want you to say fork without stuttering."

"I c-can't. You are m-making fun of m-me."

"You can, and I would never make fun of you. We are going to work until we get it right and then surprise your parents. It is something we have to keep secret until we get it right. Now let's start again."

She folded her arms, lifted her chin with a stern, stubborn look on her face, refusing to participate.

"Liza, that is not the way a princess behaves. So let's start again."

She eventually did try again and again and finally, after the fourth try, got it right. She got a little excited, and Roger said, "See, I told you, you could do it." As she gave him a hug, he said, "Now we go on," and he laid down the second fork. When she was unable to say "two forks" without stuttering, he picked them both up and laid down the first fork again. "If you make a mistake, we start over again."

After several more tries, she managed to get past two. She got excited and screamed and jumped up and down. But at that time, Roger said, "I think we have had enough for today. It's time for recess, so you can go play with Nanny as I clean up. Remember the lessons with the forks are our secret. Now run along, your mother or father will be along soon to pick you up."

Liza did not hesitate. She was up and running before Roger could finish.

In less than fifteen minutes, Jean arrived to pick up Liza. After greeting each other, Roger commented, "I see your problem with her academics. We only had a chance to work with her math skills in which we concentrated on fractions which is what they are working on now. She has a problem with the basics. Now that I see what level she is at, I hope to begin at a level she can understand. How did your job search go?"

"It is not easy. Most positions would require transportation that is not available. They are too far from home to walk to, or the hours available would not allow Scott and I to coordinate the use of the car in order for both of us to get to work and back. I don't mind walking, but sometimes it is just too far, and the time would be unrealistic. Besides, walking during winter months would be out of the question. Public transportation here in Alderwood is almost nonexistent. It leads to very limited possibilities. I have been on the phone for hours with no luck."

"Maybe I can help you out. You have a driver's license, I assume, and I have a licensed vehicle that is very seldom being used. You are welcome to use it not only for looking for work but to use to get to and from your job once you find one."

"I couldn't do that. But thanks for the offer."

"I know it is not the fanciest. But it runs good and is an automatic, so you should be able to drive it even if it is a pickup. Besides, you would be doing me a favor. I don't use it often enough. A vehicle needs to be driven to keep it running properly. As long as you pay for the gas, it is a win-win situation. I'll get the keys." And he got up from the swing where they were sitting and headed into the house.

"Wait, I didn't agree. Why would you do this for us?"

"I told you it would be a favor to me as well. You are solving a problem I have had for months." And he proceeded to go into the house.

"But—" She was too late. He was back with the keys before she could object further and placed them in her hands.

Just then Liza realized her mother was there and ran to her and gave her a hug. "Mama, I l love you."

"Yes, and I love you too. But I hear you are struggling with your schoolwork."

"I do not l-like f-fractions. They d-don't make s-sense. I don't kn-know why I h-have to learn them. And Roger w-won't let me play w-with Nanny until we s-study first."

"I'm sure in time it will make sense. Do you want to come back Monday?"

"If I g-get to play with N-Nanny, I guess."

Roger spoke up, "I told you recess comes after homework, but, yes, you can play with Nanny, she belongs to you. Now I think it is time to gather eggs before you go home."

But Jean, still holding the keys, was a little confused. How did she end up with keys for an automobile in her hand when all she came to do was pick up her daughter?

"Come on, M-Mama, I'll sh-show you h-how to g-gather eggs. It's e-easy, I'm g-good at it."

All Roger could do was laugh a little as he looked at Jean.

In her mind, Jean was thinking, *What have I got myself into?* but she went along, as Liza had taken her hand and was dragging her toward the barn.

Roger followed behind with a smile on his face. Liza was truly taking over her kingdom, and the confidence she now showed was something she had been lacking.

Once in the barn and when Liza opened the gate into the chicken coop, she proceeded to instruct her mother on how to collect eggs. "Now y-you watch me." She put her hand under the chicken in the nesting box nearest her and gently pulled out a blue egg. "This is an Ara Araucana chicken, a-and it lays blue eggs."

"I see that," Jean replied.

"Now it is y-your turn. That n-next one is…"

And she looked at Roger, who said, "A Rhode Island Red."

"Oh yeah, and sh-she lays big b-brown eggs. Be gentle, sh-she is a l little a-aggressive and m-may try to p-peck you."

She looked at Roger as if to get guidance and permission. "It's all right, she may peck at you but most likely not make contact."

"Most likely! What do you mean by most likely?"

Roger was sitting in his chair that was in the coop. He was having a hard time holding in a laugh. "Chickens threaten sometimes, but they are chickens in heart, and their pecks are only idle threats that seldom end in real contact."

Then Roger and Liza both laughed. But Jean was not amused and gave them a stern look. Roger and Liza laughed even more. What was not funny for Liza previously now was.

"Go ahead, M-Mama, she w-won't hurt you. Are you ch-chicken?" Then she laughed again.

"That is not funny, young lady," Jean said.

Roger is having a ball and having a hard time holding it in. "Sorry, Liza went through the same thing. It's my fault."

She finally got up her courage and slowly extended her hand into the box and under the chicken. As expected, he gave a peck that didn't touch Jean, but she quickly withdrew her hand anyway. She looked over at Roger, and he just gave her the nod of the head. Her second attempt was successful, and she pulled out a large brown egg. She held it up with pride on her face. Liza had set the basket on the floor, and she smiled and clapped her hands for her mother's success. They all smiled, but in the meantime, Roger picked up the Dorking and placed her in his lap. She was looking up at him and clucking.

"Well, doesn't that beat all? You do talk to chickens," Jean commented in amazement.

"I told y-you, Mama," Liza said.

"Come over here," Roger said to Jean. He then got up, holding the chicken. "Here, sit down."

"No, no, you don't."

"Trust me, it will be all right. Now sit down."

She then handed the egg she still had in her hand to Liza and slowly went over and sat down. Roger gently sat the chicken on her lap. With her eyes closed and ready to scream, Jean sat motionless. She then opened her eyes, and the Dorking was looking up at her, clucking. "Stroke her," Roger said. "She likes it."

Finally she got the nerve and did so. "She is smooth and feels good. I guess she likes me. You know this is pretty soothing and relaxing." And the chicken continued to look up at her and cluck as she settled into Jean's lap.

"Don't get too comfortable or she may lay an egg," Roger teased.

And as he saw Jean tense up, he said, "I'm just teasing. She is only being friendly, which is her nature. She will only lay eggs in the nesting box. Shall we finish gathering the eggs, or do I have to do it myself?"

Jean then gently stood up, and the chicken jumped to the floor. They then all finished the egg gathering and headed back to the house. "See," Liza commented. "I t-told you g-gathering E-Easter eggs was f-fun." Then they all laughed.

When they got to the porch, Liza was holding the basket of eggs, and Roger said, "Now you take those home. I'm sure Scott is wondering what happened to you two."

Jean, in shock, looked at her watch. "Oh gosh, I lost track of time. We better hurry home. Thank you for everything. Come on, Liza, we have to hurry." They all said goodbye and waved to each other as they rushed down the driveway.

Chapter 10

Lesson Two

The following Monday, Jean walked to Roger's and picked up his pickup. She had told Scott about the arrangement, and he, like Jean, was reluctant. But after a back-and-forth discussion, he realized the advantage it would be. It seems again a path was given that would resolve a roadblock they were facing.

She had only driven cars before but found, since it was an automatic, there was little difference. She had set up appointments and was nervous. After all, she hadn't worked since Liza was very young and Scott's grandmother was alive. She scheduled appointments to give Roger and Liza enough time to go over the planned lesson, which Roger claimed should take no longer than two hours. It was arranged for her to leave the truck at his place after each day. They didn't really have room at their place for two vehicles, plus others seeing it on their property could lead to questions. "Good luck," he said to her as she drove down the driveway, and they all waved. "Now, young lady, we have lessons to get to."

"Do we h-have to?"

"Yes, we have to. Now to review, how many quarters does it take to make a whole?"

She thought a little before answering, "Four."

"That is right, and how many halves make a whole?"

This time she answered more quickly. "It takes two."

"Very good, now that wasn't so hard, was it?" She just gave him a look of boredom. "Today we are going to apply the use of fractions in multiplication and division." He started out with the twos, explaining that every number was one-half of two. Then the threes, again explaining the fraction of one-third. He took it slow, and soon she started to see relationships and even started to cheer up and took pride in herself. After a couple of hours and she had made good progress, they switched to the practice with forks. With effort and starting over several times, she managed to get to three.

At that point, Roger said, "I think we have made progress today. Classes are over. But before you play with Nanny, I think we should gather the eggs. I want to do it before you mother gets here. I think we made fun of her enough last time."

At that Liza had to laugh, remembering how her mother had reacted to their teasing. Liza grabbed the basket that was hanging on the wall and said, "I can d-do it m-myself. You are o-old and n- need to rest."

All he could do was smile and snicker. She really was taking charge of her life, and it gave her the confidence needed to face future challenges. After gathering the eggs, she placed them on the small table on the porch, where Roger was resting on the swing, and went to play with Nanny. She was no longer the sad, sniffling child whose eyes he wiped tears from that first day. This was a child of confidence and pride, and she was taking charge of her kingdom.

He soon found that Liza learned better with the use of visual stimuli instead of the rote memorization found in the classroom environment. In the following month, they made great strides in her math abilities. They would also go over other subjects as they were assigned her in class. Her spelling improved as well as all other subjects, and her grades showed it.

Jean got a job at the local grocery store as a checker, the same position she was working at when she met her husband. It was part-time, as she wanted, in the middle of the day so she could be home to pick up Liza on her study days with Roger or be home on her nonstudy days. The use of Roger's pickup worked out perfectly.

On this Friday, Liza came running up Roger's driveway, yelling, "I got an A, I g-got an A!" She was yelling. When she reached Roger, on the back porch, she shoved the paper at him. "I got an A on my math test!" she yelled with a smile.

"I knew you could do it. Maybe we could celebrate by taking a day off schoolwork. How would you like to learn to milk Nanny?"

"C-can I? I know sh-she will let m-me."

So they grabbed the stool and the milk container and then proceeded to the coral. Roger showed her how to sit on the stool and lean on Nanny while she was against the railing to steady her. After a few tries and some spilt milk, Liza managed to get a little in the container. Roger was patient and helped hold the goat against the fence. Liza showed frustration with Nanny and scolded her with a few choice words, but they eventually learned to cooperate and work together. In the end, Liza was all smiles and held the milk up to Roger in pride. Although there was just over a glass, Roger considered it a successful endeavor.

"You go get the eggs, and I'll take the milk into the house, and I will get a set of forks for the fork lesson." They had worked on the forks every day she came, and she had managed to get through four a few times.

When she got back with the eggs, she noticed the forks were not on the little table as usual. "W-where are the f-forks?" she asked.

"The weather is getting colder, and it is getting darker sooner. Despite reservations, I am going to break one of my rules. I feel allowing you into my kitchen would be more comfortable. For lessons only, and only in the kitchen." He opened the door, and they walked in with the eggs still in her hands. "Sit down at the table. The forks are set up. I will put the eggs away. Go ahead, I can hear you."

She then started the fork lesson, "One fork, two forks, three forks, four f-forks."

"Try again."

She started again and this time got all the way through. "I did it." "Now when you go home, offer to set the table, and I want you to call them out like you did here as you place the silverware on the table. Not only with the forks but do the knives and spoons as well."

"But I c-can't, I have not p-practiced them."

"Yes, you can. I want you to practice saying spoon and knife now. The rest you already know. You are not only going to show your parents an A on your math test, you are going to show them something else. It's time we stepped things up." She hadn't noticed her stuttering had shown improvement, and he now was going to make her face it and make a concerted effort to improve it.

When Jean arrived to pick up Liza, they were sitting on the swing, with Liza practicing her silverware lesson. Of course, Liza ran to her and gave her the usual hug. "It is getting cooler out, so I have allowed Liza to study in my kitchen. I invite you to come inside so you can see for yourself the way things are. I don't want any misconceptions or misunderstandings. With the changing weather, I am afraid it will be too dark and cold to continue outside lessons shortly. Please come in. I want you to see where she will be studying, and we can discuss her progress. By the way, she has something to show you, but she wants to wait for her father to get home so she can show you both at the same time."

When they walked inside, Jean was a little taken aback with the simplicity and lack of furnishings. He still had an old woodstove in the kitchen. He did have a modern electric stove also. She found out everything was electric since there was no gas line to the house. He explained there was a small water heater in the bathroom but no furnace. There was a small bed up against the wall near the fireplace in the living room. The only other items in the living room was a lounge chair and a small desk with an old wooden chair. There were shelves over the desk, and on the desk were a computer and printer. There was no television or any pictures or anything at all on the walls. The floor was wooden, and you could tell it was the original in the house. What was originally a bedroom he had turned into a shop. The doors to the bathroom and shop were closed. The kitchen, the only room he allowed them in, had a half wall separating it from the living room. The fireplace was in the corner of the living room, adjoining the half wall. The kitchen contained the usual appliances, with the counter full of small appliances including a wheat grinder, food processor, all kinds of canning supplies, and items Jean didn't recognize. An abundance of cupboards were above, and below, the counter which extended all the around the kitchen. His simple table with two chairs rounded out items in the kitchen. He brought in the chair from the living room desk so they all could sit down.

"Mama," Liza commented, "he doesn't h-have a TV."

"I don't have a radio either. What would I need one for? I have enough to keep me busy, and I don't need to hear about the world's problems. I have experienced enough myself. Now if you are acceptable with this arrangement, I have some eggs you can take home. There may have been some extra milk if Liza hadn't managed to spill most of it."

"I wasn't m-my fault. Nanny w-wouldn't stand s-still, and she k-kicked. I got to m-milk Nanny. It w-was fun, but I g-got a little o-on me and the g-ground."

Then they all laughed a little. "She did fairly well for the first time.

I'll make a farmer out of her yet."

Jean then spoke up, "It is getting a little late, I guess we better be getting home. Thank you for allowing us into your house, and thanks again for the use of your pickup. It really makes things easier. I probably wouldn't have a job if it wasn't for it."

They said their usual salutations, and Liza and her mom walked home, leaving Roger along in his kitchen.

The minute Scott walked in the door, Liza was on him with a hug. Jean was there in a minute. "Now that your father is home, what is this important thing you have to show us?"

Without a word, Liza handed them the piece of paper she had in her hand. They looked at it together. Both hugged her excitedly, and her father put his arms around her and picked her up in his arms. "We are so proud of you." And he gave her a kiss. Jean hugged them both.

"Roger said you were smart and had faith in you. He was right. We knew you could do it too. Now you have proven us all right. Congratulations, honey, we love you."

"Mama, can I s-set the t-table?"

"Why sure, you usually do anyway. I have some things in the kitchen to finish up, and your father has to clean up."

When Liza got to the silverware, she did as Roger had told her; out loud, she set them out as practiced. Before she had finished with the forks, her mother heard her and stopped what she was doing and turned to watch her and walked to the entrance to the dining room. She finished with the forks and then started on the spoons and then the knives. By the time she got to the knives, her father was also watching and listening from the bedroom door. She had made no mistakes, and Jean was in tears before she even got to the spoons. When she finished, Jean ran to her and gave her another big hug, and Scott joined her.

"I did it, Mama. R-Roger said I c-could, and I did it."

Both her parents were in total shock. This was a complete surprise, and they didn't know what to say, so they just stood there in tears, holding her.

The next day, which was a Saturday, Liza ran to Roger's to report her success in the silverware project. "I did it. It m-made Mom and Dad c-cry. But it was a h-happy cry. Th-they said they w-were proud of me."

"I'm proud of you too, and you should be proud of yourself as well. You worked hard, and I have a present for you. Come with me to the barn."

"But I h-have been in the b-barn. Th-there is n-nothing in there ex- except chickens."

"You will see."

When they got there and he took her into the chicken coop, he said, "I know you like the Barred Rock. How would you like to name her and make her your chicken?"

"But you s-said you did not n-name them be-because you didn't w- want to get at attached to them?"

"That was because it would make it harder to end their life when the time came for them to become food."

"I am n-not a baby. I know ch-chickens are k-killed for f-food. We eat ch-chicken all the t-time. I don't w-want to adopt one and n-name it and g-get attached k-knowing it w-would end up on the t-table."

"That's the idea. If you want her as a pet, she would never end up on the table. We would allow her to live her life out naturally and die of old age. However, you have to realize she probably only has about eight years left. Can you accept that?"

"You m-mean she would be m-mine like Nanny? And we w-would never k-kill her?"

"She would be yours. But you can have another one if you prefer. You can think about a name and let me know later."

"Oh no, H-Henrietta is the o-one I want. She is so p-pretty."

"Henrietta? It didn't take you long to come up with a name?"

"She h-has always been Henrietta to m me."

"Well, Henrietta it is then. Now sit down in the chair, get some grain in your hands, and I'll put her on your lap. You can get acquainted."

She sat down as instructed, and he caught the Barred Rock and set her in Liza's lap. Although not as friendly as Dorkings, Barred Rocks are sociable and will attach to people easily. Soon they were close friends, and Liza didn't need grain to keep her on her lap. Henrietta settled down and closed her eyes as if sleeping, and Liza stroked her smooth, soft feathers.

"Now there is one more thing I want you to do," Roger said. "When you gather the eggs, I want you to count them out loud as you did with the forks. No stuttering. If you mess up, start over. When you have gathered them all and they are in the basket, count each color and say the color. You have proven you can do it. It is time for you to take charge. You are the boss. Don't forget it. I will be here if you feel the need for support, and we will keep working with new approaches. We will continue working on your studies where needed."

In the following months, Liza became ardent in her efforts. She was adamant in her attempts to decrease her stuttering and launched into her schoolwork with renewed vigor. She was at the top of her class in almost all subjects, especially math, by the end of her fifth grade. Her parents were in total awe. They could not believe the difference. They no longer worried about her, and now she was truly the pride of their lives. When they visited with her teachers at school, they too were in complete amazement. They wanted to know how they had performed such a drastic change in their daughter, complimenting them on their parenting and teaching skills.

Her scholastic endeavors were not the only improvements. She was now becoming popular in school. Although her stuttering was still evident, it had improved, and she was seldom teased about it.

She was now entering the sixth grade a proud confident student, a far cry from where she started when first moving to Alderwood.

She also had responsibilities she never had. She had two animals she loved that adored her that she was responsible for. That responsibility made her realize she could also take charge of her own life. And that attitude was one of the main factors in her success in all her life challenges. Now the Peterson house was full of joy and confidence—no more tears and unhappiness.

Chapter 11

A History Lesson

Geography was a new subject in sixth grade, and Roger seemed to be an expert in it. During the lessons, Liza soon found he had been everywhere. He had stories and pictures that brought things to life. It made her feel as if she were there herself. She did not only learn names and locations but the history, customs of the people, and a little of some of their language. She could say hello, goodbye, yes, and no in numerous languages. History came to life for her. She could visualize the naked Olympians at the first Olympics in Greece and watch the gladiators in the Colosseum of Rome. She could see the Eiffel Tower in Paris, the Great Wall of China, the pyramids of Egypt, the Leaning Tower of Pisa, Mayan ruins of Honduras and Mexico, and the wonders of Istanbul, Turkey: the only city located on two continents and countless other places. Roger's stories and pictures brought them to life, and she was often invited to share them with the class during studies. The books did not compare to the information she was able to provide.

During one of these history lessons, he asked her if she had heard of Cleopatra and Mark Anthony.

"I think I h-heard of the m-movie."

"It was not just a movie. They were real people. In fact, Cleopatra was the last Pharaoh on Egypt."

"I heard of P-Pharaohs. They were l-leaders of Egypt, b-but they were all m-men."

"That's a misconception. There were women Pharaohs. As I said, Cleopatra was a Pharaoh, and Mark Anthony was a general of the Roman Empire. The Roman Empire and Egypt were in constant conflict with each other over territory expansion. Julius Caesar—Caesar was the title of the Roman leader—and Mark Anthony fell in love with Cleopatra, and she became their lover, which prevented Rome from invading Egypt as was planned before she became Pharaoh. Anthony, the head of the Roman army, and Cleopatra built a strong relationship, but there was another general of Rome who was intent on taking over Egypt for the Roman Empire as planned. He, along with Cleopatra's sister, plotted to kill both Cleopatra and Anthony. With the support of the Roman army, Anthony was killed in a great battle in Northern Greece. Cleopatra, without the protection of Anthony, escaped to a sanctuary in Ephesus, Turkey. Everyone in the sanctuary was to be under strict protection with guards on duty at all times. But again, by deception with the help of one of the guards, in the middle of the night, Cleopatra was captured and taken out and killed."

"That was a t-terrible story. Why tell me s-such a sad s-story?"

"I want you to understand these people of the past, history, were people just like you and I. They had lives and feelings and problems just like we do. In those days, power and dominance was a way of life. By studying history, we can see what can happen if we refuse to get along and help each other out."

"Let me tell you another story. Have you heard of Hannibal?"

"H-Hannibal? That's a f-funny name. Was that a p-person?"

"Yes, he was a leader of Carthage, a country on the north coast of Africa. Again the Roman Empire was intent on bringing that country under its control. Hannibal, tired of defending his country, decided to attack Rome instead. He couldn't attack by crossing the Mediterranean and attacking the empire, Italy now, from the south since Rome was in the north, so he decided to attack from the north. He raised a large army and several hundred elephants and crossed at the narrow point between Africa and what is now Spain. He traveled overland to the Alps, a mountain range located in what's now France, Austria, and

Italy. Resistance was minimal, but crossing the Alps in winter cost him greatly in soldiers as well as elephants. By the time they finally started south toward Rome, most of the elephants and a large portion of his forces were lost. Going south toward Rome, the villages and people all under Roman control were overwhelmed by his forces, especially these beasts they had never seen before and had no defense against. Hannibal gave them two choices—join his forces or he would destroy them all with their villages and families. After heavy losses, most chose to join, and his forces grew. But he never came close to replacing what he had lost.

Especially since the elephants were the key to his success. When they finally reached Rome, there was a huge battle that lasted days and the loss of hundreds of thousands of lives. Hannibal won the battle, but by then they had been away from home over a year, fighting from their families, and Hannibal decided to go home without entering the walls of Rome. He and his forces were tired, and he had proven his point: Rome was not invincible. To this day, the walls of Rome have never been breached by an enemy army. You can still see this day portions of it throughout modern Rome."

"Is that a-all they did in the p-past, fight each other?"

"I told you this story to show you they were real people, not just storied, and they had the same desires we have. Hannibal attacked Rome to prevent them from destroying his country and families. The Romans who joined him on the way did so to preserve the lives of their families and villages. Once his point was made, he took his forces home to their families instead of continuing to attack the city and losing more of his soldiers. In those days of aggression, war was the only way to protect their families. And the protection of their people was their most important duty. We are no different. Our most important duty is to our families, and your father would fight for you as those of the past."

"But we don't h-have to fight any m-more."

"I have fought in two wars and many thousand died to protect their families. War leaves no winners. That's why we must all learn to live in peace and tolerance with each other. But we all fight our wars within ourselves, and we must fight those wars with love and joy. We have a lot to be thankful for. Concentrating on the joys and privileges we have and sharing them with others will ensure these tragedies never happen again. But I didn't tell these history events to scare or make you sad. I wanted you to understand the past was made up of real people, and these people changed history. Understanding the people of the past can help us understand ourselves."

"I liked the story of H-Hannibal. It was in-interesting, but I f-feel sorry for the e-elephants."

"Yes, man has not been kind to animals, but they have been essential for man's progression."

"You won't l-let anything h-happen to Nanny."

"No, you know how I feel about the care of animals and nature.

Now let's get back to your studies."

He related many historical stories to her as time went by, and in time, she really got into history. And as her teacher became aware of her knowledge and stories, she was asked to relate some of them to the class.

Her decreased stuttering during her presentations did not go unnoticed by most, and an A in the subject was a no-brainer. Other students constantly wanted to know more and how she knew so much. She became quite popular. She could not reveal her real source, but to avoid lying, she just said she had a friend she kept in contact with that did a lot of traveling.

Chapter 12

A Family Is Born

Some of the phrases Roger had her working on for her stuttering exercises related to her activities, such as "my chickens lay eggs" while gathering eggs and "Nanny gives me milk" as she milked her. Performing the act as she said it helped. These she mastered in a week or two, but now she was working on "welcome home, Father, I love you." And it was proving to be somewhat difficult. To practice it, she would stand on the back porch of Roger's, and he would come out of the back door. Again, words along with the association helped. But her greeting was made harder at times because he would come through the door, making a silly face or acting like a monkey or doing something else unexpected. She would just break out laughing and say, "Stop that, I can't t talk when you do that." And she stuttered very little because she was relaxed and didn't think about what she was saying. That was the point. It took about a month, but she finally got it down and received the biggest hug from her father possible when she greeted him.

Her visits to Roger's became less frequent. Now with new friends, her socializing became something new for her that she relished. She was also spending more time studying at home. One day while at his place, doing her chores, she said, "Can I call you G-Grandpa? I don't have a r-real one, and the other ch-children do, and I feel l-left out. I feel like you are my g-grandfather."

He was taken aback at first but, with watered eyes, said, "I would be proud to be your grandpa, but I am old enough to be your parents' grandpa and your great-great grandpa. But Grandpa will do just fine, princess." Now they both had a title and they gave each other a big hug. "I love you, princess."

"I love you too, Grandpa."

That day they had gone a little past their usual time. In fact, they were surprised because her mother had not returned from work to return the pickup and pick Liza up. When they walked out the back door, they found the truck parked in the garage where it belonged.

"I guess she came home late and thought you had gone home already. I lost track of time. We were doing so good."

"It's all right," Liza said. "I have w-walked home alone b-before. It's not far, an-and I'm not a b-baby, you know."

"No, you're not." And he smiled at her. "You come in and get the eggs and milk. I have something else for you." When in the house, he handed her a plain sealed white envelope. "This is for your mother, so don't open it."

"What is in it?"

"It is up to your mother if she wants to tell you."

"But, Grandpa, w-we don't keep s-secrets."

"This is not our secret. It is your mother's, and if she wishes to tell you, it is up to her. Now run along, princess, before she starts worrying about you."

"Yes, Grandpa," she said with a smile and a hug.

He hugged her back and, with a return smile, said, "Goodbye, granddaughter."

When she got home, her mother was there. "I thought you would already be home. I'm sorry, I should have checked and walked home with you. I had to work a little late."

Liza took the eggs and milk and put them in the refrigerator and took the envelope out of her backpack and put it on the counter next to where her mom was busy. They gave each other a hug, and Jean said, "What is this?"

"Grandpa said to g-give this to you."

Jean suddenly stopped what she was doing and turned and looked at Liza. "Grandpa? Since when do you have a grandpa?"

Liza smiled at her. "I asked R-Roger if he would be m-my grandpa, and h-he said he would b-be honored."

"You can't just make someone your grandpa."

"Why not? Everyone else has a g-grandpa and grandma. I need one, a-and Roger might as well b-be mine. He says it's a-all right with h-him."

"Well, I guess you two can adopt each other. Yes, I see no problem with it. But I have never had a grandparent myself, and your father only knew his grandmother who died when you were very young. But he is old enough to be our grandfather. You could be a great-great granddaughter."

"He could be a g-grandfather to a-all of us. That way y-you would have a g-grandfather too. I think he w-would like that." At that she smiled and skipped off to her room.

Jean stood there a minute, a little surprised but happy. Then she turned to preparing supper. She completely forgot about the envelope she had pushed to the end of the counter.

Liza soon emerged from her room to set the table as it had become her assignment, especially when her mother was busy or late. Each time, she practiced her silverware lesson, which never got old for Jean. It was music to her ears, and she listened with a smile on her face. Then she said, "Did you o-open the envelope?"

"I have been a little busy. I'll open it later when your father gets home."

Just then Scott walked in the front door and was immediately engulfed in arms from both females of the family. As soon as the greetings were exchanged, Jean said, "Supper is a little late. I hope you don't mind pot roast again? I had to work a little late today."

"That's all right, it tastes better the second time over anyway." At that he left to get cleaned up.

As they sat down to the table, Jean exclaimed, "The milk came from Roger's. The milk and eggs sure help with the grocery bill."

"That's all right, I am getting used to goat's milk, and the quality of his eggs is better than we used to get at the store. So what's the good news for today?"

"It appears we now have a grandfather," Jean said.

"A what?" he said.

"A g-grandfather," Liza said.

"When did this happen, and who? Oh, wait a minute, I think I can guess."

"Yes, it is Roger. Liza asked him today if he would be her grandfather, and he said he would be proud to be. And I told her he was too old to be her grandfather. That he was closer to being ours, and I guess I got carried away, and since I have never had grandparents and you don't have any, we could also claim him as ours."

"Did you clear that part with him?"

"It's all right, Daddy," Liza said. "He loves y-you too. He'll be g-glad to be y-your grandfather."

"I kind of like the idea. I have felt a little lost since Grandma died. Like something or someone was missing. Maybe he can fill that hole. Liza has sure taken to him. And he adores her. He already has done more for us than any grandfather I know. You'll get no argument from me. So I guess we have a grandfather as long as he agrees. So let's eat, I am hungry." And they all finished their meal with small talk on how the day went for each.

After supper, Scott offered to help clear the dishes, as he often did when his wife worked late, and noticed the envelope on the counter. "What is this?"

"It is something Roger—ah, Grandpa—sent home with Liza."

Liza had gone to her room. With the excitement of gaining a grandpa, she had also forgotten about the envelope.

With Liza in her room, her parents felt free to discuss adult and personal matters. Then as they were cleaning up, Scott finally said, "Aren't you curious?"

"Curious about what?"

"About the envelope."

"It has waited this long. It can wait until we finish the dishes. Then we can sit down on the couch and relax and open it together."

"Well, I am curious, but I guess I'll have to wait since Liza said it was to be opened only by you. It seems pretty thick. It must be something special."

"Don't be silly. He is always sending her home with something such as eggs, milk, honey, preserves, or some canned goods."

"But those don't fit in an envelope."

Soon they were done, and Jean picked up the envelope and proceeded to the couch with Scott right behind. As she opened it, she let out a gasp and put her hand to her head. Scott was there and saw what she saw at the same time. He just stared with his mouth wide open. Then he noticed a note with it.

Mrs. Peterson, it is time you got a decent vehicle to use for work. You shouldn't have to drive my old truck around. It is not good enough for a wonderful lady like you. You should not have to be seen in my old thing. You have a reputation, and I am sorry I didn't think of it when I offered it. Use this to acquire a vehicle becoming of you. I know it will not buy a new automobile, but you should be able to get something used that will be better than I first offered. Again, forgive my insensibility. PS. Mr. Dobson may be able to assist in guiding you to an honest dealer and getting a good deal.

They just sat there in shock, looking at each other after reading the note. Finally, Jean was able to speak. "We can't possibly keep this money. I'm going to take it back to him first thing tomorrow morning. I don't have to work."

"I agree with you," Scott said. "But let's at least count it before we return it." As Jean still sat there in shock, holding the letter, Scott was counting the money. "Fifteen thousand."

"What?" Jean said.

"There is $15,000 in cash here. That is not a 'not much.' We could buy a very nice car with that much."

Jean was furious, "I don't care how much is in there, or how nice a car we could buy, we can't keep it, and that's final!"

"But, Jean—" Scott was cut off.

"There are no buts. Give me that envelope. It was meant for me, and I will take care of it."

"For one thing, I don't see any writing saying it was addressed to you, and second, the note wasn't signed by him."

"You know as well as I do who sent it. But I don't know how to face him." By then Jean was almost in tears. She leaned on Scott's shoulder. "What am I going to do? I can't even think straight. I am so mad and yet confused."

"Calm down, I'll get off early tomorrow, and we'll go down there together before Liza gets out of school. I don't believe she needs know about this. But I can't let you handle this alone."

"Scott, I am so glad I have you. You are able to stay calm and logical. Without you, I would make a mess of things. Thank you. But I will be a bundle of nerves until we can face him together."

Scott turned on the TV, partially in an attempt to get Jean's mind off the money. And he engaged her in conversation, which he seldom did, relating to it, to distract her. They finally managed to retire with Jean somewhat calm. But she knew she would not be able to sleep.

The next day, as she was waiting for Scott, she received a phone call. "I'm sorry, honey. Something has come up at work. Albert, one of my coworkers, got sick and had to go home. I have to finish his route. You will have to go to Roger's on your own. Just remain calm and explain that we will be fine and the use of his truck has been a godsend and more than we could hope for. A newer vehicle is not necessary. Remember to remain calm, and we don't need his money. I'm sure he will understand. Just don't lose your temper, everything will be fine. I love you."

By then Jean was furious. "I can't face him on my own! I need you to explain things in a logical, calm manner. You know I get emotional."

"You will do just fine. Now I have to go. See you when I get home." And he hung up.

"But—" she started to object, but he had hung up. And she began talking to herself. "Now what am I going to do? I know this has to be taken care of today. Stay calm he says, he will understand. I don't understand."

As she walked the two blocks to Roger's place, she kept saying to herself, "Stay calm, he will understand." She hoped he would be somewhere outside, but as she reached the back porch and called for him, there was no sign of Roger. She then knocked on the back door with no answer. Panic was again setting in. She knocked again a little louder. Again a long pause without an answer, but eventually he answered. "I'm sorry," Roger said. "I was in the shop, working. And the noise of my power tools did not hear you. I'm not used to receiving visitors during the middle of the day. In fact, Liza is the only visitor I expect, and school is not out yet. She is such a wonderful child, so full of life. She has brought so much joy into my life. Is there something I can do for you?"

Jean held out the envelope. She tried to remain calm. "We appreciate the offer, but the use of your truck has been and is more than enough. We can't possibly take this."

"Wait a minute," he said and disappeared into the house. A few minutes later, he appeared with a tray of cookies and some milk. "I'm sure the walk here was a little tiring. Some cookies and milk should help."

But under the plate was another envelope which he handed to her. "What is this?" she said.

"I guess the conservative amount I gave you may have been lacking. I have been out of the market so long now I have no idea what an automobile costs. I'm sorry for my lack of insight. I didn't take into account license fees, insurance, and other expenses."

Now Jean was even more confused. "No, no, you don't understand. It isn't that it is not enough. We can't accept it because you need the money more than we do, and it's not right to take money from you. We are doing fine. You have already done more than enough for us. Liza now calls you her grandfather, but this is too much."

"Nothing is too much for my granddaughter—ah, correction, great- great-granddaughter—and that makes you my granddaughter, or something like that. So we are family, and family takes care of each other. Helping my family brings joy to me. Do you want to deny me that?"

"Of course not. But—"

"Then I don't see any problem, and there are no buts. Now, not to be rude, I think we have resolved your issue, and I have things to finish in the shop. Thanks for dropping by. I always enjoy your visits." Jean just sat there as they had been seated on the swing, with a cookie in her hand and now an open mouth. She thought to herself, *What just happened? I came here to return an envelope full of money and I am being sent home with two envelopes with money.* In the meantime, Roger had reentered the house, so he considered the issue closed.

In fact, that was his intent. He figured she could no longer object or argue the point if he was no longer present, and she would eventually take the hint and leave. He was not being rude; it was just his way of avoiding conflict.

This was one of the days Liza was not scheduled to stop by Roger's. However, she was going to stop by a friend's house to study together. Despite working late, Scott returned home before Liza, which was fortunate for her parents. It gave Jean the opportunity the chance to relate her visit to Roger's. As she expected, Scott was baffled. How could she come back with more than she left with?

"You don't understand," she said. "He confused me, and everything happened so fast I didn't have a chance."

Scott had not been totally against the first envelope of money but was now adamant on its return because it was getting out of hand, and they had lost complete control. "Give me those envelopes. I'll go down there now. You stay home for Liza. I'll straighten this out once and for all."

At that he took the envelopes from her, walked out the door, and got into the car. He sped out of the driveway, and Jean watched from the open door. He would take care of it. Scott was always calm and diplomatic. She was sure he would be able to handle the situation.

When Scott reached Roger's, he was in the coral, milking Nanny. He walked over to the coral fence and, without saying a word, just stood there, leaning on it. Roger, noticing him there, said, "This must be a special day to have both of Liza's parents visit me. I'll be done in a minute, and we can visit." When he finished the milking, he picked up his stool and the milk and walked out of the coral. "If you would like, I'll join you on the porch when I put this milk away." Soon he joined Scott on the porch. "Please sit down," he said as he pointed to the swing. "Now what brings you here? I had a visit from your wonderful wife earlier. It's a pleasure to see you both on the same day. You have a wonderful family."

"Roger, I'm not here to discuss my family. And, by the way, Liza has adopted you to be her grandfather. But again, family relationships is not the reason for my visit."

"Oh, I disagree," Roger said. "It is all about family."

Now Scott was getting confused as his wife was, but he had his argument worked out. "This is about money you offered us to buy an automobile we do not need. We are getting by thanks to the use of your pickup. If you need that pickup back, I understand, and we will make do. But in either case, you need the money as much or more than we do. Look how you have to live. We do greatly appreciate the generous offer, but we can't take your money."

He had not confronted Roger before, so his reply came as a little shock. "For one thing," Roger adamantly exclaimed, "I live the way I do not because I have to. It is because I want to. I do not need the money, as you imply, and I don't want you to just get by or make do. This is not just an offer, it is an obligation. Whether you like it or not, we are family: a family of choice, not biologic. I am free to take care of my new family in a way I choose fit. Now, since I am the elder member, I don't feel obligated to justify nor explain my actions when I feel it is for the best of the family. In fact, my happiness is dependent on being able to take care of that family and make sure they are safe, comfortable, and happy. Now do you want to sit here and argue, or do you want to go out and find your wife a nice dependable form of transportation?"

Now Scott understood what his wife had faced earlier that day. He could see they were no match for this stubborn old man. All he could do was lean over, give him a hug, and say, "Thank you, Grandpa, we love you."

They both had wet eyes, but neither wanted to cry or let the other see their emotions. Finally, Roger said, "The next time I see you, I want to see you in a new car coming up my driveway. Now get out of here, son, before I take a switch to you."

Scott just laughed, picked up the envelopes, got up, and walked to his car. They waved to each other as he drove down the driveway. They truly were a family, and it felt good.

By the time he got home, Liza was there. And Jean looked at him with a big question on her face. "Guess what, we are going car shopping." Liza was totally in shock. She had no knowledge of the events of the day. Jean knew what was going on but was also surprised. Apparently, Scott had been no more successful than she was. But it wasn't really that much of a shock. Roger was a shrewd negotiator, and he had logic on his side.

Chapter 13

Becoming One

The next week, they spent looking for a good used car after work hours. With the money available, they even considered a new one but soon neglected the idea. A good used one would be more in line with Roger's concept of economizing. Besides, as he pointed out, there would be other related expenses. By that Friday, there was a new used car sitting in their driveway when Liza arrived home. They had got a good deal, and it was only a couple of years old, but it looked brand-new to Liza. "Where did you g-get the new c-car?" she said.

"We told you we were looking for one. We picked it up during your father's lunch hour. Do you like it?"

"I like blue. It is p-pretty."

"Your dad is coming early, and we are going to go for a drive. Would you like that?"

"Can we g-go to Grandpa's? I want him to s-see our new car."

"Yes, Liza, we will be going to Grandpa's. Maybe we can convince him to go for a ride with us. Now help me set the table so we can eat as soon as your father gets home so we can go on that ride."

Liza anxiously helped set the table, and when her father came in the door, Liza ran to him and gave him the regular hug and told him she loved him. "Oh yeah," she said, "I have s-something to show b- both of you." And she ran to her room and came out with some paperwork. She handed it to them.

"Liza, this is great," Jean said.

"We are so proud of you, honey," said her father.

She had her report card. It was straight As except for one B. She also had a math test that she scored 100 percent on. She was beaming. "I didn't get a-an A in reading. But I a-am working on it."

"We have an A student," her father said. We are so proud of you. We have two things to celebrate tonight, so let's have supper and go on that car ride."

"I am n-not an A student, I h-have a B, but Grandpa s-says I will get th-there if we keep w-working on it. He makes m-me work hard."

"I think someone else deserves an A. And not just for schoolwork. Now let's sit down and have supper before it gets cold."

"All right," her husband says. "But tomorrow night we are going to celebrate properly. We are going out to eat, so don't bother fixing anything for tomorrow night. Maybe we can even convince Grandpa to join us."

The new car was a blue compact Chevy. To Liza, it was the fanciest thing she had ever ridden in. It had all the newest switches and features, and she had to try them all. Once Liza was in, Scott insisted Jean do the driving. After all, she was the one Roger gave the money to with instructions it was to be used for the purchase of a car. "Why is Mama d-driving?" Liza asked. "You always d-drive, Papa."

"This is going to be her car, Liza, so she doesn't have to use Grandpa's truck anymore for work. Don't you think she needs her own car?"

Liza just shrugged her shoulders and settled into the back seat. "Everyone buckle up," her mother said. When she got a positive response from all, she then said, "Then we are off."

As soon as the car came to a stop at the back of Roger's, Liza was out the door, ran to the back door, and, without knocking, ran excitedly into the house, calling out, "Grandpa, Grandpa, we h-have a new c-car." He was in his shop, where he usually was after dark, working on his projects.

He heard her and stopped what he was doing and came out to meet her in the kitchen. "Settle down, they can hear you clear down at the park."

"But, Grandpa, y-you have to see. It is s-so pretty, and Mama is d- driving. You m-must come and see and c-come take a r-ride with us." She grabbed his hand and dragged him out the door. Scott and Jean remained in the car, letting Liza enjoy the moment with her new grandpa. When they got to the car, Liza was beaming. "It is Mama's c-car to use for w-work. You can have y-your truck back."

Roger looked it over, and Scott stepped out and shook his hand. "Thank you, I don't know how we could ever repay you or thank you enough."

"It looks like you made a wise choice. As far as thanking or repaying me, you owe me nothing, and I am the one who owes the thanks. You will never comprehend the joy you and Liza have given me. That is worth more than all the money in the world."

Liza, not aware of the finances involved in the purchase of the vehicle, impatiently grabbed his hand again. "Come on, y-you can sit in th-the back seat w-with me."

"You know how I feel about leaving my property. I think you can enjoy a drive without me."

Scott, who was still standing outside next to him, said, "This is special. We are celebrating Liza's almost-perfect grades as well as the new car, and you are responsible for both. Now it is dark, so no one will see you. We won't be gone long. You are a part of the family, and we wouldn't feel right without you."

"Please, Grandpa, f-for me."

"That's not fair, Liza, you know I can't refuse that smile and beautiful face. Well, I guess a short drive wouldn't hurt since it is dark."

Then Liza dragged him into the back seat with her, and off they went on a late ride. They took the back road into the mountain where they knew he loved to be, where they could see the stars in the clear sky. This they did as they stopped and all got out, looked up, and gave thanks for all that had been given them.

The next day, which happened to be a Friday, they prepared to go out to eat after everyone was home. "Now where should we go?" Scott said.

"McDonald's," Liza shouted out.

"We are not going to McDonald's," said her mom. "We are going to a real sit down restaurant, not fast food."

They seldom went out to eat. It was not within their budget. But this was going to be an exception. "I've heard that restaurant on Pine Street is pretty good. Murphy's, I believe it is called. Shall we give it a try?"

"It sounds good to me," said Jean.

"I want to go t-to McDonald's," Liza responded. "Can we pick up G- Grandpa and take h-him with us?"

Jean gave her a hug. "I'm afraid that would be asking too much of him. It was hard enough to get him to go on a ride with us last night." "I've got an idea. Let's all go to his place tomorrow early and spend the whole day there. We can help him with his chores, which I'm sure there are plenty, and we can all prepare a lunch and eat there as one big—well, not so big—family," her father said.

Liza got excited. "Can we, can we?"

"I think that is an excellent idea," Jean said.

They all piled into the car and went out to Murphy's.

Early the next morning, they showed up at Scott's as he was returning to the house after milking Nanny. Liza ran to him and gave him a big hug. "Careful," he said. "You could spill the milk. I really enjoyed the ride the night before, but I am afraid right now another is out of the question."

"Grandpa, w-we came to help y-you. We are a-all going to spend t- time together today as a f-family."

"She's right," her father said. "You have helped us so much, especially Liza. It is time we helped you. Now where do we start?"

"It is not necessary. You don't have to do that."

Now Jean stepped in. "I once had a wise man tell me, 'Happiness comes from helping others, not because you have to but because you want to.' Now are you going to deny us the happiness of helping because we want to?"

They all just looked at each other and smiled. They had all had the same lecture. "I guess sometimes things come back to bite you in the you-know-what," he said. Then they all laughed.

Then Roger explained the projects he needed to get to. They divided things up. Roger and Scott took on the task of trimming the trees. Jean tackled the front lawn, trimming rose bushes and weeding. Liza took care of the animals, feeding them and gathering eggs. Of course, she had to sit and hold Henrietta for a while. But she also joined her mom in the yard work. After the tree trimming, which went fairly fast with two sets of hands, the men turned to the garden, weeding and harvesting.

After a couple hours of weeding, Jean decided it was time to start preparations for lunch. She planned to bake some fresh bread since he was out and never bought any. Everything she found had to be prepared from scratch. She found the refrigerator and pantry well stocked. However, she had to look for utensils and needed pots and pans. Liza, who had spent more time in the house, was a little help, but in general, they were playing hide-and-seek with needed items. It was a learning experience adapting to homemade butter, ground wheat flour, honey in place of sugar, and the other adaptations. But it was fun to adapt and learn. They found just enough silverware and plates for four and had to bring in the chair from the living room desk and porch so all would have something to sit on.

When Jean sent Liza out to get the men, Roger was a little surprised. "We said w-we were going to s-spend the d-day with you. I-I helped Mama fix l-lunch."

When they entered the kitchen, the table was set with four chairs, and the food was on the table. The smell of fresh bread filled the house. There were mashed potatoes, fresh vegetables, and a salad, all from the garden. Nanny's milk, as well as homemade fruit juice, was available to drink. And, of course, the fresh bread with honey, jellies, jams, and homemade butter. "We did the best we could. I don't know how you do it day after day."

"I usually eat pretty simple. This is a banquet. You shouldn't have gone to so much trouble."

"This is our first meal together as a family. I only wish it could have been more, but this was my first time working from scratch. I found it to be not only challenging but very satisfying and educational. I could get used to this."

"It looks great," Scott finally remarked.

"You have done wonders." "I h-helped, Daddy," explained Liza.

"You sure did, honey, now let's all sit down, and you can really see how good it is."

They all stuffed themselves. Roger commented that not only was this the first time in many years someone had prepared a meal for him but that it was the best meal he could remember. Jean and Liza both went over to him and gave him a big hug. "I think we should make this a regular event. You do not have to eat alone," Jean said.

"Mama, you forgot a about the d-dessert," exclaimed Liza.

"Oh, I almost forgot." And Jean went to oven and pulled out a dish of bread pudding, again made totally from items from his property.

"I am stuffed, but that smells so good. I'm just going to have to find room," Scott said. "In fact, the whole meal was so good I think we are going to come here more often. Forget about Murphy's." Then Jean laughed with him.

She said, "I think the goat milk, fresh eggs, fresh ground wheat, and vegetables fresh from the garden have a lot to do with it. But I agree, everything did seem to taste better. Maybe it was because it was prepared by my own hands. And I know it is a lot more nutritious. Now let's see how the bread pudding came out."

Despite the fact everyone claimed to be full, there was no pudding left as they all sat back and relaxed, afraid to move. In time, they all moved to the porch where three shared the swing as Scott relaxed in the porch chair he brought back out. With little talk, they enjoyed the sunny day as they relaxed until the meal settled and they could move again.

Eventually, Liza, who seemed to recover sooner, remarked, "Come on, Mama, w-we have to f-finish the weeding."

"Yes, honey, you're right." And she slowly got up.

"Hey, wait a minute," Roger said. "You have done enough. You need to leave some for me. It gives me a chance to get my hands dirty. There is a special feeling when I can commune with Mother Earth."

"Hold on there," Scott cut in. "I think we all should work together. I'm sure there are enough weeds for everyone, and the roses need trimming. Come on, Liza, let's get some clippers and more gloves from the shed, and we can work together. After all, a family that works together stays together. And I am going to take that sign out of the end of your driveway." That brought a smile from his wife. They spent the next three hours working together, and the results were amazing with a beautiful weedless rose hedge by the white picket fence. There no longer was a Roger; he had been replaced by a grandpa.

Chapter 14

Getting to Know the Animals

By now Liza was doing very well with her studies, so her visits to Roger's were cut back as she was involved more with friends and other activities. Her visits were spent with speech exercises and taking care of and playing with her animals.

A couple of weeks after the first family visit, the Petersons visited again as a family. It was again on a Saturday but was after lunch since they had things to do that morning. The purpose of this visit was not a work visit. Liza wanted to feed and visit with her animals. She secretly planned to get her parents to become more acquainted with them and convinced them to accompany her there.

When they got there, Roger was coming out of the woods with a wheelbarrow full of wood. Scott, seeing him, ran to assist him. "You shouldn't be doing this. Here, let me take that. Where do you want it?'

"I may be old, but I am not dead. I can manage."

"I never said you couldn't. But as long as I am here, there is no need for you try to kill yourself. Now where do you want it?" And he took the wheelbarrow from him.

To be honest, the gathering of the wood had worn him out, and he was glad for the help. He was just too proud to admit it. "Just put it in the shed next to the garage."

As he wheeled the wood to the shed, Liza ran to Roger and gave him a hug. She could tell he was spent and helped him to the swing on the porch where her mother was waiting.

As Scott opened the shed door, he was amazed. It was full of all kinds and sizes of wood. "What do you do with all this wood?"

"Woodworking, as you know, is my hobby. I cut it down, plane it, and shape and finish it to work into my projects. Unusable pieces or leftovers I burn in my fireplace or woodstove. Nothing is thrown away."

By the time he had unloaded everything, closed the door, and put away the wheelbarrow, Liza had said her greeting and was off to the barn. "I said to feed them," Roger said. "Not play with them." However, he knew it would do no good. Her pets were the joy of her life, and telling her not to play with them was like telling the sun not to rise. So even saying so, he had to laugh a little. He knew she would feed them, but she would also spend time in play. In Henrietta's case, sit and hold her as they talked to each other. He then turned to her parents. "You better follow her. You may have to end up gathering eggs as she forgets once she has Henrietta on her lap or her arms wrapped around Nanny's neck." And at that, they could hear Nanny bleating in her pen next to the barn.

When they got to the barn, Liza anxiously showed them where the feed was and how to feed Nanny and the chickens. They just looked at each other and, with a shrug of the shoulders, did as Liza demonstrated. As was usual, Henrietta walked up to Liza and started clucking. Liza bent down and picked her up, holding her in her arms. Jean and her husband completed feeding the animals as Liza continued to hold, talk to, and stroke Henrietta. Nanny continued to bleat, trying to get Liza to pay attention to her, so Liza handed Henrietta to her mom. "Here, you t-take her. She l-likes you. Nanny is h-having a fit. I better g-go play with h-her. She gets so jealous."

Jean had held the chickens before, so she was not disturbed or afraid. She even liked petting them. However, Scott was unfamiliar with them, and she decided to play a joke on him. "Sit down on that chair over there," she indicated. "You look a little tired from unloading all that wood."

"I am fine."

"Just sit down," she said, a little more forceful.

He was confused, but when she used that tone of voice, he knew he should obey, so he sat down. Then she started to cluck. He just assumed she was talking to the chicken in her arms. He had been told they talked to you and seen Liza do such, so he thought nothing of it. However, Jean was not talking to Henrietta. Soon a chicken jumped up onto Scott's lap, and although he didn't jump up as Jean anticipated he might, he was in complete shock and a little fearful. Jean just laughed.

"What's so funny? I got a chicken on my lap, and you're laughing at me."

"It's all right, she won't hurt you. That is the Dorking Liza told us about. You made fun of her. Now the table is turned. The Dorking is very friendly and likes to be held and stroked. I have held her, and it is pretty relaxing. Try it."

Cautiously he placed his hands on the hen and slowly drew his hand over her back. She responded by looking up at him and clucking. Then she settled down and closed her eyes.

"This is amazing," he said. "I promise not to make fun of her anymore."

"Oh, that's all right. She doesn't care. She just wants to be paid attention to." Then they both chuckled and continued caressing their chickens.

About then Roger walked into the barn. "It seems gathering eggs is an all-day job for you two. Do you need help?"

Jean responded, "I guess we got a little distracted. We haven't gathered them yet. I'll get right to it." She dropped Henrietta and picked up the egg basket.

Scott stood up, and his chicken flew to the floor. "I'll help."

Roger just laughed. "Like daughter, like parents. She is a chip off the old blocks. But there is nothing wrong with those blocks. And there is nothing wrong with connecting and showing compassion with nature's creatures. In fact, it shows a sensitivity we all should have and express. That is one of the things that makes Liza so special."

"Special," Scott said. "Most people's children have a dog or cat for pets. Mine has chickens and a goat. I guess special is one way to consider it."

"Well, at least she doesn't have a rhinoceros. That might be a little hard to hold in her lap." Then they all laughed as they finished gathering the eggs.

They heard a concerned yell from the coral. "Mama, Papa, s-something is wrong w-with Nanny." Jean put the egg basket down, and they both rushed out to see what the yelling was about. When they reached Liza and Nanny, they found Liza rubbing Nanny's belly.

Despite that he had never even spent time with Nanny, Scott stood back and said, "She looks fine to me."

"She is not f-fine. Look at h-her, she is g-getting fat. She has been the s-same since I kn-known her. This is n-not normal."

"It is if you are pregnant," Roger said from the barn door he was leaning against.

"She is g-going to be a m-mother?" asked Liza in shock. "How did that happen?"

"Well, I guess your education in animal husbandry has been a little lacking."

"I know h-how animals get p-pregnant. But she is by h-herself without a h-husband."

"I guess now is as good a time as ever to give you another lesson in nature. Goats only give milk for about eighteen months after giving birth to a kid. If you want them to continue to produce milk, they must continue to produce young at about eighteen-month intervals.

So Nanny is going to be a mother in about three weeks. She is just fine."

"You m-mean we are going to h-have a baby goat!" Liza responded excitedly.

"Baby goats are called kids. But, no, when Nanny gets close to deliver, I will take her to the farmer where I got her and where I take her to become a mother. She will stay there for about a week after giving birth so she can nurse her kid with the special milk she will produce so it will be healthy. Her milk at that time is not that good anyway, and the kid needs it. After that, he has other goats to nurse it or that give milk he will use to feed the kid. She may miss her offspring at first, but with your loving friendship, in a few days, she will be back to normal.

"But that is m-mean to take her b-baby away. Why can't y you keep it? I would t-take care of it."

"I know you would. But that is the arrangement I made. He gets all her kids until I need a replacement for Nanny and then I would get another nanny for free."

"But we h-have Nanny, and you g-gave her to me. I wouldn't n-name another goat N-Nanny, and you are not g-going to get rid of Nanny!" she said emphatically.

"Liza, Nanny is yours, and we will never get rid of her until her time comes. We have been through this before. There is a time for birth and a time to die for all living things. Goats, like all other animals, do not live forever. Nanny is still young. She has several years ahead of her. She will probably outlive me."

Liza then gave Roger a hug. "Grandpa, I don't want you or Nanny to die."

"We have discussed the cycle of life before. We can't change it, but we can use the time given us to make things better for others during our time and those who follow. Now no more talk on this subject. We are now expecting a new life, and that is something to celebrate and find joy in."

Liza's parents just stood back, holding each other, listening to the two, glad they were not the ones to have to cover the subject with their daughter. Liza then gave Nanny a big hug. "I love you, Nanny, y-you are going to be a m mother. I'll take c-care of you. Mama, Papa, come a-and give Nanny a l-love. She needs to k-know we will t-take care of her."

Jean had been with Nanny before and didn't hesitate, but her father had never had contact with the goat previously, and he cautiously approached. Roger laughed a little. "Most animals, including goats, don't act or feel any different when pregnant. In fact, until a few hours before giving birth, except when there are complications, they do not act any different than normal. After birth, in most cases, they are back to normal within an hour. Nanny doesn't know she is pregnant and will act as she normally does. And she doesn't need any more attention or care than she usually gets and will want to play as you usually do."

With that, the game of tag began, and no one was exempt. There was the tagging and butting laughing and running around. Even Scott got involved, and there was no more talk of death and sadness.

As the weeks passed, Liza's speech improved greatly, Jean learned to milk Nanny, and Scott started to help Roger around the property, making repairs and keeping up the property in general. Fresh eggs, goat's milk, preserves, and other canned goods were a staple of the Peterson table. Nanny did go and have her kid, at which time Liza missed her greatly and would just stand against the fence for long periods of time.

On one of their visits, Jean commented on the drabness of the inside of Roger's house. "Why are your walls so bare and the inside so drab? We need to lighten it up a little."

"It is fine the way everything is. There is nothing I need on the walls to take care of and straighten. I don't spent time looking at my walls, and I have no one to impress."

"But you have such beautiful roses outside. Why don't you bring some inside to freshen and brighten up the place?"

"Nature is more beautiful outside, and that is where they belong. To bring it inside would mean killing it. We need to protect and enjoy nature the way it was meant to be, not destroy it for our own selfish wants."

Chapter 15

One-on-One Meeting

On one of those days when her husband was at work and Liza at school and Jean had the day off, she decided to visit Roger. Nanny was not back yet, and she felt like having a one-on-one visit to get to know him better.

When she knocked on his door and he finally answered, he said, "I wasn't expecting you or even Liza today. Are you here to help, or is there something I can do for you?"

"I am here just for a friendly visit, but if there is something I can help you with, let me know. But first of all, I would like to thank you for the diplomatic way you handled Nanny's pregnancy situation a few weeks ago. And I would also like to apologize for the comment last week of the drabness of the inside of your house."

"I didn't feel the need to go into female animals going into heat and the fertility process or the sex process to her at her age. We have discussed a lot about nature, but those detailed topics should be left up to parents. As for the comment about the interior of my abode, there is no need to apologize. I know it does meet standards of most households, but since I have no visitors, I don't feel obligated to meet those standards. Simple is my standard. As for a friendly visit, I would enjoy the company, as long as you don't mind me continuing my canning as we talk. I am canning beans. If you don't mind, you can cut the ends off and cut or break them in pieces. I don't like to can whole beans. Here, I'll show you how. I'll take care of the jars. They have to be washed and scalded along with the lids and rings. Then I'll fill them. I like to add a little salt to the water. Then they have to be processed. You can watch as you work, and soon you'll be an expert. It will go a lot faster with the two of us working. So what do you want to talk about?" he said as he showed her how to cut the beans.

"I just want to really get to know my new grandpa. I know you gave me a pretty good description of your character, but I want to get to know you. For one thing, I like the idea of having a grandfather since I never had any grandparents. It is amazing what you have done for Liza. But what is it that persuaded you to take such an interest in her?"

"I consider myself a good judge of people and emotions. I could tell from the minute I met her she needed a friend. She was a sad individual, and not just because of what she went through at that time. I could also see through the tears in her eyes the strong spirit of someone crying to get out. Seeing another in the distress she was going through brought out the same pain in me. That is one of the reasons I choose to live as I do. I, for some unexplained reason, can feel emotions of others, especially if they are strong even when they try to hide them. It got to the point I was sad all the time because of others, and I couldn't do anything about it. This time, I decided I would do something, or at least try to do something about that hurt that I was also sharing. I don't claim to know all the answers, but sometimes it doesn't take answers. It takes understanding and a listening ear. To be honest, I didn't intent to or expect to see her again after that day. But I at least felt better after she left and think she did to. And that was enough for me."

"But that wasn't your last encounter with her, and she became enthralled with you. And when she met Nanny, she was hooked. She always wanted a pet, but we just couldn't have one. In fact, she loves animals in general. But you have interrupted your whole life to not only help Liza and all of us. Why?"

"The love of animals is very common in people, especially children, who are lonely and sad. As for why do I continue to help all of you? Selfishness. To be honest I, like Liza, was a lonely, sad individual, and assisting you made me feel better about myself. I think I have already made it clear, not only to Liza but your whole family, that true happiness only comes from making others happy. And I truly believe that."

"But helping is helping. You have provided a substantial amount of money with no strings attached. No one does that without something in return."

"Well, I guess you just called me a nobody. But I have received a return—joy and happiness and the satisfaction that I have helped someone who deserves a break."

"But why are you so devoted to her well-being?"

"As I said, I could see she was very special. She has brought so much joy into my life. She is a ray of sunshine. In a way, she saved my life, and I can't repay you and Scott enough for sending her to me."

"But we didn't send her to you."

"I believe you did. It was your choice to move here. It was your choice to move to this neighborhood. I do believe, to a certain degree, in fate, and I think we all needed each other, and now you are stuck with me."

During their conversation, they continued the canning and, in fact, were almost finished without realizing it. When Jean finished cutting the last of the beans, she went over to Roger and gave him a hug and said, "I love you, Grandpa, and you're stuck with us."

When she left Roger's that day, she left with a smile and peace of mind and a feeling everything would be all right. They would never have to move again or worry about finances or the future.

Chapter 16

The Broken Window

Three months into her last year of grade school, Liza came home furious. She had stopped by Roger's after school and saw him working on the front porch of his house where he was working on a broken window.

"Some kids are s-stupid and mean!" she said after arriving home. "What's the matter, dear?" her mother inquired. "Did something happen at school?"

"Not at school. Some high s-school student threw a r-rock through Grandpa's window."

"Unfortunately, some of the older students still consider the property haunted. Remember he told us about the vandalism that went on before and after he moved in? Roger is still considered strange by many, and children can sometimes do cruel and mischievous things. It happens."

"B-but it isn't right."

"You ought to know by now that a lot of things in life aren't fair or right. We just have to deal with them in a calm and peaceful attitude. Remember how he handled things when you first met? I'm sure Grandpa will do as usual and take care of things in his usual calm way. We have to let him handle things and stay out of it."

But Liza would not stay out of it. She immediately got on the phone to some of her friends to see if they knew anything about the incident. Some of them had older siblings in high school that may have been walking home with those who were responsible. With the town being as small as it was, the high school and middle school were located next to each other, so some of the middle school students may have even been present. After a few calls, she found out the individual who threw the rock was a sophomore in high school by the name of Andy Christianson. As well as anyone knew, he had no brothers or sisters and lived alone with his mother.

A friend of hers had a brother who was a high school student and walked home that day with the group Andy was with. He had related to her what had happened that day. He wasn't sure what led up to the rock throwing, but he said Andy showed reluctance at first.

When Liza's father came home, she was still upset. She relayed the incident and what she had found out to him. Her mother overheard her relaying the topic and cut in adamantly, "Liza, I told you to stay out of it."

But her father said, "I'll go over and see if he needs help fixing the window."

"I'll go with you," Liza exclaimed.

"No, you won't," her mother said. "Your father can handle it."

Liza just folded her arms and gave a *humph*.

When Scott arrived, Roger was still working on the window. Without a word, he stepped in to help. The replacement was almost complete, but Scott helped with the calking and cleanup. No words were spoken during the work, but when the cleanup was completed, Scott spoke up, "Liza told me about the window, I'm sorry. She is very upset and managed to find out through friends the name of the individual responsible. If you would like, I would be willing to go talk to the parent. Apparently, he lives with his single mother. I'm sure she would like to know or at least should."

"Children will be children. It isn't the first time I have had to replace this window. In fact, I had a spare just in case. That is how I was able to get to it so quickly. Thanks for the help, however. This is something I would like to take care of in my own way. But I may be asking your assistance."

"Just let us know what you want us to do. Liza is pretty upset. I don't think she will let it go so easily."

"That is one of the things about her that makes her so special. But tell her to forget it. As I said, I will handle it. Although I don't want you involved, if you could possibly obtain the address of this young man, I would appreciate it."

"I'll see what I can do, and I'll do what I can to convince Liza to stay out of it."

"Thanks again for your help."

"Considering everything you have done for us, it is nothing. I'll let you know what I find out."

At that they said goodbye, and Scott went home to his family. As soon as he entered the door, Liza was on him. "How did i-it go? Are you going t-to have Andy arrested?"

"Liza, you don't arrest someone just for breaking a window, especially a minor," he replied.

"But h-he has to be p-punished and made to p-pay for damages."

"Grandpa will handle it. He says we are to leave it to him. That's means you staying out of it!" he said with force and a wiggle of his finger in her face.

She stomped off to her room. "We will be eating in ten minutes, Liza," her mother said.

Quietly Scott relayed to Jean the discussion he had with Roger and his request to find out the address of Andy.

"I suppose I can ask around. I have gotten to know some of the regulars at the store."

"No, he wants everything kept quiet and private. Since he was walking on this street, Andy must live close by. That means it is in my work area. I have the names and addresses of everyone on the route. I can check for a Christianson in this area."

"But isn't that a breach of privacy. Does the company allow it?"

"I need the information for my job anyway for billing, and I am not divulging anything to the public. But he said he didn't want me to even give him the information, so I am not giving out the information to anyone."

"But that seems strange. How is he going to handle it if he doesn't know the address?"

"You should know by now strange is nothing unusual when it comes to Grandpa."

She had to hold back a laugh, concerned Liza would hear. "So we'll let him handle it, like he asked."

But letting things go was not in Liza's nature. The next day after school, she confronted her mother. "Mom, if I h-had done something to c-cause damage to the p-property of someone else, w-wouldn't you want to know?"

"Liza, you were told to stay out of it."

"But if I did, wouldn't you want to know?"

"Yes, Liza, we would. And I'm sure Andy's mother does too. But that is between Grandpa and her. Now I am not going to tell you again, stay out of it!"

"But, Mom!"

"There are no buts. Grandpa will handle it. Now get cleaned up and do your chores so we can eat as soon as your father gets home."

When Scott arrived home, Jean met him and indicated to him, with a finger to her lips, to be quiet. "Liza is having a hard time letting this window breaking go. I'm afraid she may do something I don't think Grandpa would approve of."

"I'll talk to her again. By the way, I got the address." And he handed her a piece of paper with an address on it.

"What am I supposed to do with this?"

"I don't know. But I understand you don't work tomorrow. I want you to go to Grandpa's and tell him we have the address as requested. Then the next move is up to him. Now I better go talk to Liza." He then went to her room, knocked, and entered. "It appears you are still troubled about Grandpa's broken window. You know how private he is. He told me he also wants this to be kept quiet. He said he would take care of it in his own way. He doesn't want you involved in any way. Now I think we owe it to him to respect his desires. I want you to promise me you will do as he wishes, agreed?"

With her head down, she reluctantly replied, "All right."

"That's my girl. Now let's get ready for supper." And he gave her a big hug.

After Liza had left for school and Scott to work, Jean went to Roger's as agreed. As she did not see him outside, she knocked on the back door. He was in the kitchen, so he opened the door immediately. "Come in, I was just cleaning up after breakfast. Is there something I can get for you?"

"No," Scott said. "You requested the name and address of the boy responsible for your broken window. I have it for you."

"I believe there is some misunderstanding. I don't want it. I want you to have it. I don't want to know his name or address."

"But I don't understand. What am I supposed to do with it?"

Chapter 17

Consequences

He then walked over to the counter, opened a drawer, and pulled out a plain white envelope. "I want you to deliver this to his mother."

Now Jean was even more confused. She knew about the plain white envelopes from Roger. "Grandpa, what are you doing? You do not reward someone for bad behavior."

"Are you telling me how to handle my own affairs?"

"You are a strange person, but I have learned by now you have a reason for everything you do. I don't understand it, but, as I told Liza, we have to respect your wishes." Then she took the envelope from his outstretched hand.

She decided to deliver the envelope right away since she had the day off and was already in the car and had the address. However, when she knocked on the door of the address she had, there was no answer. Then she remembered Mrs. Christianson was single and most likely at work. So she put the envelope in her purse and planned to deliver it that evening. She didn't want to hold on to it any longer than she had to.

When Scott arrived home, she had him join her in their bedroom, showed him the envelope, and explained the day's undertaking. He was just as shocked as she was. She tried to get him to deliver it, but his argument seemed logical. "I believe as a single mother it would be best if another woman delivered it. I think you can connect better than I could. Besides, she might be threatened by a man confronting her with her son's criminal activity. She may not even be aware of the incident."

"What you say makes sense. But that doesn't make it any easier. Maybe we could go together?"

"You know as well as I that if we went someplace together without Liza this evening, there would be a lot of questions and a discussion neither of us want. We will just tell her you had an errand to run, or better, you forgot something to pick up when you went to the store today."

"But she knows I shop on the days I work there."

"We'll make up something. We have to get out there before Liza suspects something."

When they exited the bedroom, Liza was setting the table, totally unaware of her parents' dilemma. After supper and they all cleaned up, Liza went to her room without a word. Jean grabbed her purse and coat and was out the door, leaving it up to her husband to make up an excuse.

When she knocked on the Christiansons' door, this time it was answered by a young man about fifteen. "Hello," Jean said. "May I speak with your mother?"

He yelled, "Mom, it is someone for you."

A woman in her midthirties came to the door, wiping her hands on an apron she was wearing. "May I help you?"

"Hello, Mrs. Christianson. My name is Jean Peterson. I live a few blocks away towards the park. Is there someplace we can speak alone?"

Jean could tell Andy, who was in earshot, became very nervous. "May I ask what this is all about?"

"I have something for you, but I would rather discuss matters in private."

"Does it have something to do with my son?"

"Yes, it does. And as his mother, I accept it is your obligation and right to handle things in your own way. However, because of the delicacy of the matter, I feel you should be informed of the situation privately before discussing it with your son."

At this point, she became quite confrontational. "Andy, my son, is the head of this household, and if there is anything concerning him to be discussed, he should be present."

"Mom, it is all right," Andy cut in. "I'm pretty sure I know what this is all about. I did something the other day I am not proud of. I threw a rock though a window and broke it."

"Andy," his mother said in shock. "What are you saying? That is not like you. What made you do such a thing?"

"You know I want to be on the baseball team. It is the only possible way to go to get a scholarship and go to college. I was walking home with some of the members of the varsity team with the captain. He said if I could prove I was as good a pitcher as I claimed, he would make sure I got on the team. He challenged me to break the window to prove my talent. I told him no at first. But with the ribbing from other team members and his insisting he would make sure I wouldn't make the team unless I could break the window, I gave in. I know it was wrong but was too ashamed to tell you. I'm sorry."

"I am ashamed of you, and whatever this woman plans for your punishment for breaking her window, I plan to double. I must apologize for my son. Andy, I want you to apologize, and you will make restitution."

Jean now spoke up, "Mrs. Christianson—"

She was cut off. "It is miss. I have been divorced for ten years. And you can call me Beth."

"Well, Beth, I am not here to ask for restitution, and it was not my window. The punishment is totally up to you. The incident has and will not be reported to any authorities. The owner of the house involved wished me to give this to you. I am only a messenger. I have been requested to deliver this to you. To be opened only by you alone and out of the presence of your son."

"But I don't understand," Beth replied.

"Please just do as requested, and maybe you will." And she handed her the envelope. "So now that I have delivered the package, I'll wish you a good evening. It has been a pleasure to meet you." And with that she turned and walked out the door that had never been closed.

Beth just stood there in shock, holding the envelope she was now afraid to open. After walking to the door to make sure it was closed, she turned with her back leaning against it. "Andy, could you please go to your room for a minute and let me figure this out?"

When she finally opened the envelope, she found a note and another sealed envelope inside it. She first read the note which said,

> Please read this before opening the inside envelope. You don't know me and I don't know you and that is the way I want it left. However, a situation has arisen that, at least for now, links us. The contents of this envelope is to be set aside to assist in college expenses for the young individual I assume is your child. That individual, at no time, is to be informed of the contents of the envelope, nor where it came from. If there is a question, it will be up to you to convince him or her. I leave it up to your discretion to handle this affair, but remember your child is to be unaware of the situation. I request privacy, so no further contact between us is desired. Good day.

Jean returned home relieved. It was over. She was relieved to be home, and to top it off, Liza, who was still in her room doing homework, didn't even know she was gone. There was no more discussion of the topic. The rest of the evening was spent in a relaxed atmosphere, and everyone went to bed in a good mood. The next morning, they all woke up feeling well rested and planned to visit Roger for a couple of hours, then go on a relaxing drive to the mountains to enjoy the fall leaves.

Just after breakfast, the phone rang and Liza answered it and the person on the other end asked to talk to Mrs. Peterson.

"Mom, it's for you."

"Hello, this is Mrs. Peterson."

"Hello, this is Beth. Is it possible to meet with you today, preferably at your house? I am uncomfortable and confused with the envelope and its contents. Andy is at a friend's house, playing, so I am free to get away now."

"My family was just headed out for an outing, but I can meet you at your place in five minutes."

"I guess that will be all right as long as Andy doesn't come home while you are here."

Then Jean turned to her husband and told him to take Liza and go to Roger's, and she would meet them there later. He agreed, and she got back on the phone. "I'll be there in five minutes."

She hung up, and Liza said, "Who was th-that, Mama?"

"It was a new friend I recently met, and she just wants to discuss a few things. It shouldn't take long. I'll meet you at Grandpa's in no time."

At that she grabbed her coat and ran out the door.

"I didn't kn-know Mama had a n-new friend."

"I think she mentioned her to me a couple of days ago. I think it is someone she works with. Now get your jacket, and let's go to Grandpa's."

When Jean arrived at the Christianson's, Beth was standing at the open door before she got out of the car. Beth was waving at her to hurry into the house. When they were in the house and Beth had looked around to see if anyone had seen them and closed the door, Jean said, "What is this all about? I thought we went over everything yesterday."

"Do you realize what was in that envelope you gave me?"

"I told you it did not come from me and was sealed when I got it. I have good idea of the contents, knowing who it came from, but, as I said, it is no longer my concern."

Then Beth handed her the letter. "Here, read this."

"I would rather not. As I said, it is something between you two, and I know what he feels about his privacy."

"Well, it is a letter to me, and I give you permission to read it and, in fact, request you read it."

At that Jean reluctantly took the letter and read it. "I read nothing out of character of the author. And it seems pretty straightforward. What is it you want of me?"

Then Beth handed her the envelope. "Count it. I don't call this out of character. I call this insanity."

Then Jean counted it, and it came to $10,000. "It's a lot of money and should be helpful with Andy's college expenses. But it is not out of character, and he not insane. I admit he is strange, but not insane. He is very calculating and has a purpose for everything. Believe me, there is no mistake, and he is quite serious and sincere in what he put in the letter."

"But I, we, can't keep it. I can't possibly accept a reward for bad behavior. Not only because I feel it is wrong but I feel totally uncomfortable with it."

"Beth, if you read the letter, it is not meant as a reward. How can Andy feel he has been rewarded if, as directed, he is never finds out about it?"

"But you have to take it back."

"Believe me, that is not an option. He knows what he is doing, and when he decides to do something, no one will change his mind. Take it as intended—a gift towards the future. Just set it aside into a college fund and forget about it until needed."

"Are you sure? I still don't feel comfortable, but you know him better than I. Ha, I don't know him at all. But I guess I'll do as you say. Thanks for coming over. You are apparently a lot better at handling stressful situations than I am. Thanks again. Sorry for interrupting the scheduled day with your family."

"It's okay, they are waiting for me. Glad to help. Now if you don't mind, I will join my family. Goodbye."

She walked to the door and opened it as Beth thanked her again and closed it behind her.

Chapter 18

Santa Claus

Things got around to normal after the broken window incident was resolved and forgotten. Although some activities slowed down on the farm, as they referred to Roger's place, harvesting and canning took top priority. Jean now became a major assistant to this activity, and canned fruits and vegetables began filling the shelves at the Peterson home. Another fall project was the gathering of wood from behind Roger's property. This became the job of Scott. The wood was not only for the fireplace in the living room Roger used for heat but for the wood cook stove in the kitchen he preferred to use. Roger usually accompanied Scott into the woods, instructing him as to what pieces were to be collected. They knew he liked to use a variety of hardwood in his hobby, but most wood would be cut up for firewood. Scott did the heavy work, cutting the pieces in the woods and hauling it back in the wheelbarrow, but Roger would cut it down and finish it up with his tools to meet his needs.

He spent a lot of time in his storage shed, where he kept his wood. There he sorted it out into piles Scott did not understand. Cutting the selected wood for firewood was also part of Scott's duty, but any wood selected by Roger for his woodworking hobby was strictly under his supervision. These he spent cutting, shaping, and sanding before taking them into his shop, the room that was built as a bedroom.

They never really knew that much about what he did in there or just what he made because he kept the door closed. However, they did know he made toys and other finished items but didn't know what he did with them. Some of the finished projects were scattered around the living room where he also had a small desk he sometimes worked at. Some of the items included plaques, clocks, or varying types as well as several finished items. The small desk was used mainly for printing and computer projects.

The Petersons were also busy with their own Christmas preparations, including cutting down a tree from the woods behind the farm, shopping, and decorating the house. Previous years, the mood for Christmas was lacking, but this year, thanks to the welcome events, they were going to go all out. That left Roger plenty of private time to spend in his shop.

Jean enjoyed walks in the fresh winter air with the sprinkling of snow covering everything. She was enjoying herself, thinking how lucky they now were and how things had turned out. She was walking home from work, and grade school had just let out. As she was passing the park, she noticed a group of children and some adults gathered around a park bench. Her curiosity brought her to approach. She soon realized they were gathered around an individual dressed in a Santa Clause suit. As she got closer, she could see he had a sack and was handing out items to the children.

Being that they had only lived there only three Christmases, this was something she hadn't observed before, probably because in previous years, she was not in the mood to take a walk in the cold weather. Her curiosity encouraged her to draw closer, and she heard a woman exclaim, "Timmy, you know there is a limit of only one. Please give the other one back."

But Santa said, "It's all right, Mom, I know he already had one, but I also know he has a younger sister who is in the hospital, and the other one is for her."

The woman answered, "How did you know that?"

His simple response was "Have a Merry Christmas," and he returned his attention to the others gathered around.

Jean approached the woman with her son as they left the bench. "Excuse me? Who is that giving things to the children, and what is he giving them?"

The boy answered, "That is Santa, can't you tell?"

Jean was about to say something when the boy's mother signaled her to keep quiet. Timmy, why don't you go play on the swings a little before we go home?"

Timmy wasted to time. He took off at a run. "I'm sorry, he still believes in Santa. I know he is a little old, but he gets to excited each year, and a little imagination never hurt anyone. To answer your question, he just started showing up about five years ago and shows up every year for a few days the week before Christmas. No one knows who he is or where he came from, but the children love him and look forward to him every year. He refuses to work for any commercial establishment or do private appearances for a fee. This is his only appearance and then he disappears again until the next year. The items he gives out are wooden Christmas tree ornaments. He seems to have an unlimited supply and a large variety, so each year you get a different one. As I said, the children love him, and the ornaments are the talk of the town this time of year."

"And no one knows who he is? How is that possible? I notice no one is taking pictures."

"Frankly, no one cares who he is, and he does not allow pictures. We respect his wishes. He does not want publicity or any form of recognition. He says, 'Christmas is the spirit of giving and the love of each other.' He encourages them to love, respect, and obey their parents as well other adults. If a child appears to be sad, he spends extra time with them, and, at almost all times, they come away with a smile. No one knows what he tells them because he talks to each privately in a low voice so others can't hear. All the parents look forward to his visits because they know he will bring back the joy many of them lose throughout the year."

"But what about candy canes that other Santas pass out?"
"Apparently, his elves, as he says, only make wooden items in his shop,

not candy. But some of the children do not come because they only want candy. He says he is here to spread joy, not cavities. Excuse me, I must get Timmy and go to the hospital where my husband is with our daughter. Nice talking to you. Have a Merry Christmas."

Jean wondered why Liza hadn't mentioned this Santa. She would have to ask her. With more observation, she thought she saw something familiar with this Santa. Because of all the children and adults gathered around, she could not get close enough to get a closer look. She then realized the time and knew she had to rush home. Liza would beat her home if she didn't hurry. Time had gotten away.

When she got home, Liza was already there. "I'm sorry. I should have been home for you. It was such a nice day I walked to and home from work and got distracted when passing the park. Did you know there is a Santa Claus who visits there every year just before Christmas?"

"Other children h-have mentioned it. Especially around this time of y year, but I'm too old to b-believe in a S-Santa Claus, so I never v-visited him. Besides, I don't like c-candy canes."

"But he doesn't hand out candy canes. He hands out handmade wooden Christmas tree ornaments. And another thing, no one knows who he is. He insists on his privacy. There is something familiar about him."

But Liza was not really paying attention to her mother. "Jan got a new d-dress today, and she invited me o-over to look at it. May I g- go over to her p-place for about th-thirty minutes? She w-wants to show it o-off. I'll be h-home for supper."

Jan was a good friend she had made that lived only a few houses away on the same street.

"Make sure you are home before your father. You know he wants to eat as soon as he gets home and cleaned up."

But Jean could not get the park Santa Claus off her mind. And despite her promise, Liza did not beat her father home. Jean again presented her encounter at the park with him as he was cleaning up.

He finally responded, "I have heard about him but never seen him myself. I never really gave it a thought since Liza and we have never believed in the myth. Why are you so interested in this Santa Claus?"

"I'm not sure. He just reminds me of someone."

"Well, when you figure it out, let me know. Where is Liza?"

"She's at Jan's. She promised to be home before you. I will give her parents a call."

Just as she got off the phone, she yelled out, "I figured it out!"

"You figured what out?" Scott asked.

"Santa Claus is Roger. I know I didn't get close enough to get a good look at him or hear his voice, but it makes perfect sense."

"Don't let your imagination get away."

"But it all adds up. We know he makes wooden items in his shop, and he keeps it closed. The month or so before Christmas, he spends hours in there. He wears a long white beard. And he insists on his privacy. He is Santa! He fits the description to a tee."

"I'll admit you present a strong case. But even if he is this Santa, it sounds as if he wishes to be so anonymously. Even if we suspect it, and I'm not totally convinced, we have no right to divulge our suspicions. You know how he values his privacy, and it seems, if your guess is right, this is another aspect of his life he wishes to keep a secret. We should respect his wishes as we have some of his other issues he feels obliged to keep secret."

"I know you are right, and I would never mention my suspicions to anyone else. But it is something else about him that makes him so mysterious."

"Promise you will not mention it to anyone. Not even Liza. We do not need any more rumors or mysteries. Case closed."

About then, Liza came in the front door, and things proceeded as normal. That Christmas Eve, the Petersons presented Roger a new shirt, which he desperately needed. They were sure he hadn't had a new one for several years. When they presented him with the shirt, he handed a wrapped present to each Jean and Liza with the instruction not to open until Christmas morning. He presented Scott with a wooden homemade tie rack, which was unwrapped.

"I'm sorry it is not wrapped. It is a little big and awkward to wrap. I hope you don't mind?"

"It is beautiful, and I don't blame you for not wrapping it. It makes it even more special thinking I may have collected the wood you made it from."

"You are correct in your assumption, and that makes it special for me too. Merry Christmas to all of you."

After their hugs, thanks, and goodbyes, the Petersons returned home with their gifts, which they placed under their tree awaiting Christmas morning. Liza opened her gift first. It was a jewelry box with her name inlayed on the top. Also inlayed was an image of a goat. It was made of various hardwood of different natural colors. There were three drawers in the front, and when she opened the lid on the top, inside there was a wooden Christmas ornament in the shape of a snowflake. Jean just looked at her husband with the expression of "I told you so," and they just smiled at each other. Liza hugged it closely with a big smile on her face.

"It is so b-beautiful. And look, Mama, th-this is Nanny. I now need to g-get some jewelry to p-put in it. Open yours, Mama."

When she did, it was similar to Liza's. However, her name was on the top and a red rose instead of Nanny. Inside was another Christmas ornament. This time, in the shape of a star. "I guess we both need some new jewelry. They are so beautiful."

"I recognize those woods. Roger has been teaching me the different varieties. They all have different features as well as colors. He would have me collect specific pieces. Now I know why he was so selective. I would never have imagined the beauty that could be produced out of the variety of raw pieces of wood. I know understand his fascination with woodworking and the love he puts into it. These are not just handmade gifts. They are a labor of love."

They knew Roger would not join them for a Christmas dinner at their house, so they took dinner to him. Again hugs and thanks prevailed, and all enjoyed each other's company. Nothing was brought up about Santa Claus. But there was no question in Jean's mind who the park Santa was, and she was sure Scott was in complete agreement.

Chapter 19

A New Friend

A week into the school break, the Petersons heard a knock at their door. It was in the evening and everyone was home and they had finished cleaning up after dinner and were just relaxing and watching TV. Scott answered the door. "May I help you?"

Jean recognized them. It was Andy Christianson and his mother. "Beth, Andy, what are you doing here?"

Beth was the one to speak first. In a low whisper, she said, "I'm sorry, I know we had an agreement, but Andy can't let it go. He feels so guilty it is affecting his relationships and schoolwork."

Scott and Liza, who had never met them before and were not familiar with the details of arrangements, were a little confused and surprised. Jean took things into her hands. "Please, Beth, would you join me in the kitchen? Andy, would you please take a seat? Oh, this is my daughter Liza and husband Scott. We'll be back in a minute, and we can all get acquainted."

She led Beth into the kitchen and keeping things in a whisper. "I thought we had an agreement and you understood. Did you tell Andy about the money?"

"No, I would never do that. I know I make a promise, but I can't convince Andy to let it go. He is a sensitive child, despite what his actions indicated. And he did not make any agreement. He feels he must make restitution, and without it, his whole attitude has suffered. He can't concentrate, and his studies are suffering. College will not be an option if things do not change. And in that case, everything your friend planned for would not happen, and I would have to give the money back. What can I do?"

Beth was almost in tears. Jean gave her a hug. "It's all right. We will work things out. But we will have to let Liza and Scott in on the situation, and your benefactor must still remain uninvolved. Now let's go introduce everyone."

When they returned to the living room, it was very quiet. The TV had been turned off, and everyone was sitting around afraid to say anything or not knowing what to say. Jean could tell Liza was not in a good mood. She knew who Andy was even though she had not met him previously and still carried a grudge. She also could not let things go.

Upon entering the living room, Jean again took over. She then introduced Beth and Andy to Liza and Scott. She did not have to fill them in on who they were, but they were confused as to why they were there. Beth finally spoke up, "I know what was agreed to, but my son Andy feels so ashamed of his actions he must not only apologize but wants to make restitution. I told him the individual he committed the action against didn't require either and wished to forget the matter closed."

Andy cut in, "Mother, I can speak for myself. I am not a child even though I acted like one. But that is not me. I am not going to make excuses, but I was coerced into something I know was wrong. I accept complete responsibility and want to not only apologize but make amends in any way possible. Please don't judge me too harshly, but I need help."

Scott spoke up, "Young men make mistakes. People make mistakes. I think we have learned firsthand that it is not our place to judge. Liza, because of her close relationship to this individual, has also had a hard time coming to terms with things. I think it is about time we all shake hands, give each other a hug, and do as our friend would want us to do. Andy, the individual whose window you broke, does not hold you responsible, and he definitely does not expect restitution or an apology. If he were here, he would say we all learn by mistakes and that is all it was a mistake, and he knows you have learned by it. That will make you better, and knowing that is enough for him."

"But how do you know that?" Andy said.

"Believe me, we have had talks, and he makes his feelings pretty clear. He has no ill feeling towards anyone. He only wishes good will towards others, and, as I said, if he were here, he would give you a big hug. But privacy issues prevent him from personal contact."

Now his mother spoke up, "Andy, do you remember that letter he sent?"

"I remember. But you wouldn't let me read it."

"There was a reason. And I can tell you what Mr. Peterson says is in line with what was in the letter. Believe me, this individual's primary concern is for your well-being, and hopefully, someday you will fully understand how much."

Liza finally spoke up, "I'm sorry, Andy, I g-guess I have not been p practicing what I have learned from our f-friend. Can you f-forgive me?"

Then Andy realized who Liza was. She was the "stuttering girl" everyone made fun of when he was in middle school. He now felt even more ashamed because at the time, although he never made fun of her, he laughed when others made fun of her. "You owe me no apology. In fact, I should apologize to you. It appears misjudgments lead to unhappy situations in a lot of cases. Please forgive me."

"For what?" she said.

"For laughing when others made fun of your stuttering. It was wrong, and I am ashamed. Can you forgive me?"

"Andy," she said, I guess w-we all have a lot to l-learn."

And she went over to him and gave him a hug.

"Liza," her mother said, "would you please go get some of those cookies we made today? I think it is time for all of us to get acquainted." They then spend the rest of the evening getting to know each other, and the topic of the broken window never came up.

In the following weeks and months, the two families became close friends. Liza and Andy, at times, walked home together. With him around, somehow she felt safer and more comfortable. No longer a loner, she had real friends and not just girl classmates. Andy's grades improved, and he also was performing better in baseball. His attitude improved, and his performance and relationships showed it.

He was able to help Liza with her studies as well, and they enjoyed each other's company. One of the subjects Andy really struggled with was history and geography. He had a hard time remembering names and events.

Roger had continued to tell Liza stories of history events. As always, he made them come to life with real events, pictures, and stories. It seemed he was telling them as if he were there as they happened, and at times she believed he was. He had visited the sites and was able to provide detailed information not available in books. It seemed he had been everywhere. These stories and details made it easy for Liza to remember facts and was becoming a history expert. When she became aware of Andy's problem with the subject, she began relating these events and stories to him. Like Liza, they made him understand the reality of history and the effects of the events. They no longer were stories bur life events that changed the world. When you could see societies as real people and locations as real places, it all came to life in a way that made it hard to forget. Soon his grades improved, and he no longer was afraid of being denied a scholarship because of poor grades.

Upon graduation, Andy did get his athletic scholarship and graduated in the top ten of his class. Liza and he and their parents became close. Both being only children, they developed a bond that gave them a sense of belonging they never had before.

Chapter 20

Raising Chickens

The months went by with nothing special to note. Liza was in her second year of middle school when Andy went off to college. She missed him, but they kept in touch. At this point, she had decided she would also work toward going to college, and Andy was very helpful in supplying her with processes and requirements necessary.

Roger was showing signs of slowing down, and Liza and her parents spent more and more time taking care of him and his place. He insisted he could take care of himself, but they made sure their help was subtle. It became a game. He enjoyed their company but insisted on taking care himself, and they knew he needed help but made the excuse they just wanted to visit. The care of the animals was an essential matter since they needed daily care, and Roger, at times, forgot or was unable to care for them.

One day Roger expressed the need to raise more chickens. His hens were getting older, laying fewer eggs, and he would need new hens to take their place. At that time, they would become meat for the table. It was the natural process on a farm, and Liza had been advised years earlier, so she was prepared. Henrietta, however, was her chicken and, as promised, would evade the axe.

Roger pulled Liza aside one day. "I'm sure you have noticed the egg production has fallen off. We have been through this before, and we knew the time would come. Most professionals and farmers use incubators to keep the eggs warm until they hatch. But we are going to do it the old-fashioned natural way. How would you like for Henrietta to become a mother?"

By now Liza's stuttering had almost disappeared. "I think she would make a great mother. How many children can she have?"

"Well, as you know, she can't lay all the eggs herself. We will have to give her some from some of the other chickens, and they have to be fertile. I think we will give her eight and see how many develop.

There is no way to tell how many are fertile and hatch, but usually six or seven should reach maturity."

"Can she sit on that many?"

"I have seen a hen hatch over a dozen at a time. That isn't the problem. The problem is getting her to nest. She has her box and should nest as long as she has an egg. So we can't take any of her eggs, and we will add to them when she leaves to eat. She may lay two or three of her own. But chickens aren't too bright, and she will adopt all in her nest."

"Can I select the eggs from the other hens to get the ones I want?" "Of course, that is part of the fun of raising your own chicks. It is also exciting to see them hatch and grow. It makes you feel a sense of accomplishment as well as a closeness to nature. Now we have to get Henrietta to cooperate."

The next few days, they collected eggs from hens Liza selected. She selected an Araucana for the blue eggs. She also liked the dark-brown eggs of the Barnevelder and the friendliness of the Dorking. The Rhode Island Red was also on the top of the list. She had to have a Silkie because she thought it looked funny and was the only hen that laid white eggs. It became hard for her to choose, and she ended up with ten eggs.

"You do realize that, just because we have ten eggs, we won't end up with ten hens even if they all hatch. Chances dictate close to half will be roosters, leaving us with only about five new hens."

"I didn't think of th-that," Liza exclaimed.

"Would you like to select another hen to raise another clutch? If we do that, we should wait another week to let them catch up. We have used almost all the eggs that have been laid. It will also give us the opportunity to make sure Henrietta will accept her new family."

In two weeks, they selected another hen to nest. This time Liza chose eggs from the Plymouth Rock as well as some of the ones she selected before. Naturally, they could not take any from Henrietta, so Liza hoped she laid more than one of her own.

Liza checked Henrietta and the other nesting hen every day. She was so excited to see the new chicks she couldn't wait.

"Take it easy, Liza," Roger told her. "You know it takes about three weeks for the eggs to hatch. Your checking every day will not speed up the process. Nature has its own schedule." "I know, but I can't help it. This is so exciting."

"I hope you're as excited when it comes time to harvest the ones that are roosters?"

Liza gave him a sour look. He just gave her the look that said "this is serious."

Twenty-two days later, on schedule, nine eggs hatched from Henrietta's clutch. The colors ran the gambit, so a good variety was assured. However, the sex was yet to be determined since only experts could determine it at this stage, and Roger did not claim to be that experienced. At this time, it didn't matter anyway. The next clutch arrived two weeks later with seven hatchlings—all that she sat on. Again there was a variety. But they knew none of them belonged to Henrietta.

To Liza's surprise, the mother hens, including Henrietta, were quite protective of their chicks to begin with. In a few days, however, they seemed to relax. Their brood followed them around, pecking at the ground next to them. Liza couldn't help wanting to hold them. But they were fast, and the mothers showed disapproval of her attempts. She did manage to capture a couple and assumed they were offspring of the Dorking because of their nature.

"Don't get too attached," Roger warned her. "In about eighteen weeks, we will have to separate the hens from the cocks and then some unpleasantness will result."

"But they are so cute. Do we have to?"

"We have been through this before. You are well aware of the cycle of life and how it works. You don't have to take part of be present. Your father and I can take care of it. It will be some time before we know how many new hens we end up with. So until then, be careful who you get attached to."

But Liza couldn't help herself. Soon she could tell some apart from the others and, despite her better judgment, gave them names. They even began to follow her around the yard to her delight and laughter. Her parents also laughed as they watched her. Roger's misgivings and warnings of getting attached were ignored. He finally gave up and enjoyed Liza's joy and laughter with everyone else.

By the end of the school year, all the new chickens were mature, and the hens were laying. The roosters, as was normal, became aggressive toward the hens and fought among each other. It was time to dwindle their number to only one. Fortunately, the hens had outnumbered the roosters almost two to one, and the harvesting of only five roosters was required. As it turned out, it was not as upsetting to Liza as she thought it would be. Mainly because they were not friendly, and as they got older, she lost her attachment to them. She still was not able to watch. There was fried chicken, chicken soup, and other chicken dishes on both tables as well as some in the freezer. All a part of the nature of a small farm, as Roger's place was considered.

Chapter 21

Happy Thirteen

That Christmas was, as usual, a busy time for Roger. The snow was heavier than the average year, so more time was spent on removal at the farm. The extra snow presented a problem for Roger as he now, at times, used a walking stick he made. Getting around became a little dangerous. Jean and Scott knew the reason he spent the extra time in the shop before Christmas. But this year, they noticed his time there consumed almost all of his time. They suspected the snow probably had something to do with it, so they didn't think too much of it or mention anything to him or Liza. Liza was still ignorant to her parents' knowledge as to the identity of the park Santa, and they agreed to keep it that way. They felt Roger would divulge the information in his own time. As far as they were aware of, he didn't know they knew.

Liza's birthday was March 16. And this year, she was turning thirteen. Her parents planned to have a birthday party for her. They would invite Beth, Jan, a few other friends from school, and Andy if he could get away from college. They were going to invite Roger as well but had little hope he would accept.

They were a little confused when Roger continued to spend most of his time in his shop after Christmas. When confronted, he replied, "You know woodworking is my hobby. Why shouldn't I be working in my shop? It's what I do."

Not thinking, Jean commented, "But Christmas is over."

"What has that got to do with it?"

Jean realized her error. She had to think fast. "But you have never spent so much time in your shop after Christmas before."

"The weather has not been good this year, and I don't feel spending time outside. Besides, how do you know what my schedule in the shop is?"

She was feeling trapped. Scott came to her rescue. "All she is saying is we are concerned about you. You can spend as much time in your shop as you wish. In fact, I would like to spend some time in there with you. You have built an interest in me for woodworking. I know you could teach me a lot."

At that Roger relaxed a little. "I think I would like to pass on my craft, but not at this time. And as for my well-being, I am fine."

They almost forgot the reason for their visit. "Oh, I almost forgot," Jean said. "This Saturday is Liza's thirteenth birthday. We are planning a birthday party for her. There will only be a few close friends, and we were hoping we could convince you to attend."

He just turned and looked at her. He didn't say a word, but they knew his answer. "We had to ask, Grandpa. Liza would not forgive us if we didn't. We love you, and, after all, you are part of our family." To their surprise, he then did answer, "I will be there in spirit. I love you too. You will always be my family. Nothing will change that, but I am still not ready to associate with others."

"Let us know if you change your mind. You know you are always welcome. It would mean a lot to Liza."

They then gave each other hugs and said their goodbyes as Roger returned to his shop. On Friday, the day before Liza's party, Roger asked Scott to come to his place to pick up a present for Liza. When he got there, there was a large packaged item of about three feet by one foot and a foot high sitting on the porch.

"I want you to take this to Liza for her birthday."

"What have you made now, Grandpa?"

"It is for her birthday present. I'm not going to tell you now. Just take it home in your car. It is a little big for me or you to carry it there."

"I know she would want you to give it to her yourself, but I will be glad to take it home for you." When he got home, Scott decided to put the box in his and Jean's bedroom. He wanted to surprise Liza with it after she opened the rest of her presents. He knew anything from Roger would be special and should be saved for last.

As people arrived for her party, she was surprised to see Andy with his mother. "Andy, you came." And she gave him a big hug.

"I wouldn't miss my little sister's birthday as she becomes a teenager." Their relationship had developed to a point that they considered each other brother and sister, and their actions showed it. Being the first to arrive avoided an explanation of the relationship to others.

Jan was the next to arrive and two other girls from school arrived together shortly after. Liza looked for the arrival of one more. "Liza," her mother whispered to her, "we invited him, but you know how he feels about being around people. He did say he would be here in spirit and to send you his love."

She turned to her guests, and everyone sang "Happy Birthday" to her as cake and ice cream was served. When she opened her presents, they were clothing items, beauty aids, and the normal items a young teenage girl would be expected to receive. As she opened the last present, it was clear that even though she enjoyed them and thanked everyone, there was a sadness to her as if something was missing. Then her father said, "Liza, I have one more present for you."

He went into the bedroom and brought out the item he had picked up the previous day. When he brought it into the living room, everyone wondered who it could be from. And even though Scott did not say who it was from, Liza knew. There was no card and was covered in cardboard under the wrapping paper. Everyone was full of questions and suspense. "Who is that from?" Jan asked.

It took a little work to remove the cardboard covering. But with Andy and her father's help, they finally exposed a wooden boxlike cedar chest. It was made of alder with the large letters spelling L, I, Z, and A inlaid in black walnut in the top. The legs were carved in an intricate design that flared to look like feet. Everyone was full of oohs and aahs and questions. "Where did it come from?"

"Who gave that to you?"

"Who made that?"

"It is beautiful."

Those were some of the comments, and Liza finally answered, "It is from a special relative."

One of the girls said, "But I thought you said you didn't have any relatives except your mom and dad."

Scott stepped in to help, "We just discovered someone we didn't know about. He is a distant grandparent."

That seemed to satisfy things, at least for now. But both the Petersons and Christiansons knew who that relative was and smiled. Liza was lying on the box and hugging it as she said to herself, "He didn't forget."

Then her schoolmates started yelling, "Open it!"

So Liza stood up and slowly lifted the lid. It was not empty as expected. Inside was a crimson silk blanket. When unfolded, on one side was Liza's name stitched into it in the center. At the corners were squares with sown figures of a goat on two corners, and a chicken on the other two corners. Under the goats were the words "Nanny," and under the chicken "Henrietta." All the stitching was sewn in very meticulously with white stitching for the goat and black and white for the chicken. After her mother helped her hold it up unfolded for all to see, Liza grabbed it and wrapped herself in it with tears in her eyes. "It is so beautiful."

Now there were even more questions and not just from her schoolmates. "Who is Nanny, and who is Henrietta?" They were all confused. Liza spent the rest of the time with a smile on her face and the blanket wrapped around her. Andy and his mother lingered on after Liza's friends left.

"This special friend, or relative, you have seems to be very talented. Is this the same individual I am indebted to?" asked Beth, in a whisper, to Jean as they were in the kitchen. Andy was still unaware of his mother's arrangement with Roger, so she didn't want him to hear.

Andy had, however, done some checking on his own and knew who Roger was but honored his desires of privacy. He did not know anything about the college fund contribution, but he still felt obligated to honor and befriend him when the time was right.

"Yes, it is," Jean responded. "But I didn't know he could do anything like this. You know how secretive he is. He just keeps surprising even us."

Andy and Liza were on the couch, talking, with Liza still wrapped in her new blanket when Beth came out of the kitchen after cleaning up. It was mostly small talk of college, but Andy expressed curiosity as to her newfound relative. His mother finally came over to him and told him it was getting late and time they went home. She hadn't had time to visit with him alone since his return home.

After Andy and Beth left, Liza turned to her dad. "Did you know about this?"

"I knew about the present because I had to bring it home, but I had no idea what it was."

Jean said, "We knew about his beautiful woodworking abilities, so the chest is no surprise, but this blanket. I didn't know he even had a sewing machine, let alone had the ability to do something like this."

Liza, still with the blanket around her, said, "This is so beautiful and soft. How did Grandpa do it?"

"I don't think we will ever now all his secrets or abilities. Maybe that is what makes him so special and interesting. But I know one thing— I'm glad he is our grandpa," Jean said.

It had been a long day, and they placed the chest at the foot of Liza's bed. She finally fell asleep with the new blanket wrapped around her.

Chapter 22

The High School Years

By the time Liza entered high school, Roger's place had become a second home to the Petersons. They were there helping most of their free time, and not because they had to but because they wanted to. In fact, it was hard to keep Liza away. She still enjoyed his endless stories and information. She got attached to the chickens, even though she knew she shouldn't. Nanny had two more kids that Liza never even got to see.

Jean got more involved in the canning and enjoyed the time she spent with the one-on-one time they had together. Roger finally opened his shop to everyone, and Scott became his apprentice. Roger found even more joy as they became teacher and student. When Scott made a mistake, he was surprised when Roger just laughed. He never got cross. He just said mistakes lead to perfection. Scott soon got into the hobby, learned to correct mistakes, and even came up with some of his own ideas.

The fact that he was the park Santa was not a secret within the family any more. Even Liza realized it when entering his shop. "I have Santa for a grandpa," she exclaimed when she found out. But she couldn't tell anyone. They also found out he did have a sewing machine in the shop and he knew how to use it.

They all shared in the upkeep of the property, gardening and harvesting. Scott did the repairs with help and advice from Roger. The animals and their care fell upon Liza. They all worked together as a family, and they found the simple life did bring rewards in the form of happiness and peace of mind.

At the beginning of her junior year, they figured it was time for Liza to get her driver's license. Liza obtained the manual to study for the written test, and as usual, Roger took it upon himself to help her study. He quizzed her on questions and, as per his teaching method, usually made a game of it. It worked to relax her, and she passed the test with flying colors the first time.

She now had a learner's permit, so the actual driving training fell to her parents since Roger would not leave his property to do so. However, that did not stop him. He would have her sit in a chair and pretend to be driving. He would make the sounds of the car, screeching tires, all the while giving her directions and situations. He would tell her there was a red light ahead, give her turning directions, and tell her the traffic conditions. Made sure she checked the rearview mirrors, used the brake, used turn signals, and any other actions called for. At times he would yell out, "Child chasing a ball across the street" or "car running red light at intersection" or some other unexpected event. When she messed up, he made the sound of a crash. At first his yelling made her even more nervous. But he sat in a chair next to her, and when she crashed, he would fall over in his chair, causing her to laugh. In time, she became more relaxed as Roger ratcheted it down and things became serious. He felt putting pressure on her at first would help her handle unexpected situations. If she learned to handle fabricated stress, she would be better prepared to handle it in reality.

When her father took her out on the road, she did very well. The two methods combined worked. Again, after putting in the required driving hours, she passed the driving test the first time with ease.

She insisted on leaving the DMV, driving directly to Roger's with her father as passenger. He was waiting on the back porch. And she jumped out of the car and ran to him. "I did it, I passed." And she showed him her driver's license and gave him a big hug.

"I'm proud of you," he said. "But I didn't doubt it a bit. You were a good student. Now get back in that car with your father, and get home to show your mom." Then he walked to the car and whispered to Scott. "Come back later without Liza. I have something for you."

When they got home, Liza, still excited, ran to her mother with the license in hand and a smile on her face, and they gave each other a big hug. Then she turned to her father, who had just stepped out of the car, and asked, "Can I take the car to Jan's? I want to show her."

That gave him the opportunity he needed. "I think that would be fine, just be careful." When she had got back in the car, he turned to Jean. "Grandpa wants to see us."

"What about?"

"I don't know. He just said to come over without Liza."

So, without any more questions, she went in the house to get her purse and a jacket. When they got to Roger's, they just walked into the back door, as was common practice now, and he was sitting at the table with an envelope in his hand.

"Oh no," Jean exclaimed. They already had become familiar with his white envelopes.

But before they could say anything more, Roger spoke up, "This is for Liza to purchase a new car, or used as the case may be. But she is a minor, so it will be up to you to make the decisions and arrangements. I know you know what you are doing since you have been through this before."

"But, Grandpa, Liza does not need a car. We have two, and that is enough. You have to stop doing this."

"She does need her own car. Soon she will be going off to college and then it will become necessary. She might as well get it now to avoid the hassle later. Do we have to go through this dance again? You know how it is going to end up. Besides, your old car is becoming undependable and will need replacing."

At that Jean and Scott looked at each other and gave a sigh of surrender. When they opened the envelope, they counted $20,000.

And when Jean opened her mouth to object, Roger cut her off, "I don't want to hear anything more. And there is nothing more to discuss. When you feel comfortable letting Liza know, you three go car shopping. Now get going or I'll take a broom to you both."

They knew there was no use arguing, so they just gave him a hug and said, "Thank you, Grandpa" and walked out. On the way home, Scott turned to Jean. "When we need a new car, we are just going to go get one. We can afford it. But if he finds out we are in the market for one, he will insist on paying for it."

Jean just laughed and said, "Agreed."

In the next two weeks, Jean and Scott shopped for a car for Liza. They wanted to find suitable options before Liza got involved and her excitement got her carried away. In fact, they were not going to let her know the money for it came from grandpa, even though they knew, eventually, she would figure it out. Liza made her choice from the five they had narrowed it down to and, to their surprise, never asked where the money came from. Scott made all the financial negotiations and financing, which was cash, and Liza was so excited she never asked questions.

Crimson being her favorite color, she chose a red four-door sedan, which, of course, was previously approved by her parents. She did not hesitate to drive it to Roger's to show it off. He just said, "So your parents bought you a car. You deserve it." Again she never suspected his involvement, and that's how he wanted it.

Liza became one of the top students in school. Her stuttering was a thing of the past, and her popularity with other students had grown, partly because she had a car of her own. Teachers also became impressed with her. With the encouragement of fellow students and teachers, she ran for class president and won.

Andy had returned from college after Liza's freshman year. He was a great aid in helping her in college prep classes and helping her decide on course selections and applications. He also encouraged her to get involved in school politics, explaining colleges looked favorably for a well-rounded student. Another incentive she had to run for class president. Once in, she found she enjoyed it. She now felt there were no limits—a long way from that shy sad child who first moved to Alderwood.

But it was not all work and studies. One afternoon, Roger, Jean, and Scott were relaxing in the swing, watching Liza milk Nanny. Nanny, for some reason, was not being very cooperative. She kept kicking and had spilled the milk once. Nanny just kept bleating "na, na, na," and Liza answered, "Na, na, na to you too."

Roger yelled to her, "I thought by now you would have been able to teach her to say her whole name. I guess she will always be a stutterer."

Liza gave him a dirty look, grabbed the stool and milk bucket, walked over to the porch, set down the stool, and walked to the swing where she proceeded to pour the milk over Roger's head. Scott and Jean, who were sitting to each side of Roger, leaned away to keep from getting milk on them. They also opened their moths in shock. Roger just grabbed Liza and hugged her as the bucket fell to the deck. He vigorously rubbed her head, messing up her hair. "I love you, monkey," he said. And then he started laughing as he hugged her even more. There was very little milk in the bucket, which was now empty, and they all started to laugh together.

Jean finally stood up, still laughing. "I'll get a towel and clean this up." As she came back with the towel and wiped everyone off as best she could, she took Roger's hand and pulled him up. "Here, let me help you up so I can wipe the rest off of you, old goat."

"Who are you calling an old goat, you Nanny?"

That just brought out more laughter from everyone. He pulled her down with him onto the swing, which he and Scott had recently remodeled to make it more comfortable and larger to accommodate four people. They had become, no doubt, one little happy family, comfortable with each other.

This incident was only one of many memorable moments they enjoyed as they became closer during Liza's high school years. During this period, Liza not only became comfortable with herself but with school and other students. Jean now felt a part of a family she never had, with responsibilities and privileges of a mother and daughter. Scott was learning from a father he could not only look up to but who also showed him respect and love he never had. For once he felt confident in himself, knowing someone was there to support him and guide him. They were ready to face anything this world threw their way.

Chapter 23

College Acceptance

Andy had graduated from Hopkins University with a degree in political science and a minor in government. Upon returning home, he obtained employment in a supervisory position in parks and recreation. He took an active role helping Liza preparing for and filling out applications for colleges and scholarships. One of those was for Hopkins University. They even took a trip there where he showed her around the campus and introduced her to some of the faculty. They found out the university had a good college in the field of study Liza was interested in pursuing.

As it turned out, Liza received a number of acceptances and a couple of scholarship offers. One of those was from Hopkins University. Although they did not offer a full scholarship, it did cover all tuition. She would still have to pay for housing and books. With Andy's encouragement, she accepted that offer and made preparations to enroll. She still had to finish high school, however, but now the pressure and suspense was over, and they all celebrated.

To do it, the Petersons planned announcing it to their adopted grandfather by taking a meal and celebratory cake to his place. They invited Andy to accompany them since he had been a big help with the applications, recommendations, and all phases of her acceptance and decision.

When they arrived there, Roger was resting on the back porch on the swing. It was late afternoon, and he had finished milking and taking a rest. As he saw them get out of Liza's new car with their hands full of food items, he asked, "You didn't tell me you were bringing supper over tonight." It was not unusual for them to eat meals at his place, but usually they prepared it there as well. And they always planned it with him ahead of time. They had invited Andy to join them, and as he exited the car last, Roger commented, "And who is your new friend?"

Andy knew who Roger was and his relationship, but was unaware of the gift he made to his college fund. Roger, however, had no knowledge as to the identity of Andy. As requested, he was never informed of who the person was that broke his window.

Liza walked to him, locking arms with Andy, and answered, "This is my brother Andy."

Roger was a little taken aback, and Liza could see it. "He is my brother the same way you are my grandfather, and he is here to help us celebrate."

"And what is it that we are celebrating, princess?"

She then pulled out the acceptance papers to Hopkins University. "I am now an official college student, thanks in great part to Andy's help." Liza let out a little scream as she and Roger gave each other a big hug.

"Well, congratulations, college student Liza. And welcome to my humble abode, Liza's brother Andy," he finally said as he and Liza broke their embrace. They had both worked toward this goal, so it was as much an achievement for him as her. "Come in, everyone. I'm sure we will have to warm up the food so we have time to talk and I can get to know your new brother. Son, will you get the chair from the shop?"

Roger and Scott had developed a very close relationship, and now the shop was shared by both. Scott had grown to not only accept Roger as a grandfather but relished their relationship. Roger had come to call him son, and it made Scott feel the love it was intended to suggest.

Scott and Jean both looked at each other with questions in their faces. They were not expecting this warm welcome for Andy, considering his attitude of privacy. Scott headed for the shop, and Jean turned on the oven to warm things up and, with Liza's help, set the table. There was a routine they had since they often shared a meal at Roger's, but it was going to be a little crowded this time. To Roger, however, adaptability was a virtue, and this was no exception they couldn't handle.

Standing for any length of time was hard on Roger, so he pulled up a chair away from the table to be out of the way. "Bring a chair over here, Andy. I think we should get to know each other since we are now related." Everyone let out a little snicker. The kitchen was small, and there was no way they could have a private conversation. "Now tell me a little about yourself."

Andy was a little apprehensive. He didn't know what information he could divulge, so he looked to the Petersons for help. There was a slight pause in what they were doing, with no one talking. So he knew he was on his own. "I graduated last year from the same college Liza will be going to, with a degree in political science, and I work for the city. I live with my mother a short distance from here. I have no actual siblings but consider Liza a sister. She was able to tutor me while I was in high school, which helped me improve my grades and gain a scholarship. I plan to get into politics, to do what I can to make this town crime-free and a community anyone would be proud to live in."

"Liza, I like this new brother of yours. He has ambition and goals to be proud of. You have made a good choice, and maybe you have found another great grandson for me."

The Petersons gave a silent sigh of relief, then laughed. They were in total shock of Roger's immediate acceptance of Andy. This was a new grandpa they had never seen before.

When Roger asked how Liza and Andy met, they said they met while walking home from school. Finding they both were only children and that Andy was struggling in school with a subject Liza appeared to be an expert in. One thing led to another. They knew they had to be careful about the true events, but luckily, Roger never pressed the issue. He was content to discuss Liza's college acceptance. They then had a good meal and cake to celebrate. There were the usual stories and teasing and laughing all around. The evening ended with everyone happy and in a good mood. After the hugs and usual goodbyes, even from Andy, they got back into the car to depart. As they waved, Andy spoke up, "I am so ashamed."

"For what?" Liza asked.

"For what I did. He even called me his great-grandson. He said he respects me. How can he respect me after what I did?"

Jean spoke up, "Andy, the past is the past. Roger doesn't know you are the one who threw that rock, and even if he did, he would not treat you any differently. He doesn't hold grudges, and he doesn't judge. What you see is what you get with him. Forget it, he has. I hope someday you will know the whole truth behind that incident and then you will really understand."

"What whole truth?"

Scott felt obligated to try to cover for his wife's slip. "We are the ones to get involved. It is in the hands of only two people."

"I am not a child. I am a grown man, and I think I have a right to know. I can handle it."

"Yes, you are a man. And as a man, it is up to you to act like one and respect and honor others' pledges. It is up to you to face things head-on if that is essential for you. As Jean said, even if he knew you threw that rock, he would not have treated you differently than he did this evening. He always says we learn from mistakes, and I think you are living proof. Bad things sometimes lead to good outcomes. Believe me, we know. Now let's get you home. It is getting late, and your mother will be wondering what happened to you. There will be no more discussion, topic closed."

Andy took the hint, and he never brought it up again. But he did relay to his mother the events of the evening, leaving out the discussion in the car on the way home. He actually did feel a part of another family, one with a grandfather. He went to bed with a smile on his face but a question on his mind.

Chapter 24

The Ultimate Gift

The next week, on a Wednesday, there was a knock on the door. Jean, who was not working that day, and home alone, answered the door. She had just gotten back from Roger's. "May I help you?"

"Yes, my name is Mr. Williams, and I have some documents that was determined should be delivered in person. Are you Mrs. Peterson?"

"Yes, I am. What kind of documents are they?"

"I am only a courier. I have no knowledge of the contents. Would you please sign here?" And he handed her a receipt to sign.

Jean signed the receipt confirmation and handed it back with a question on her face and mind. "Thank you," the courier said. "Have a nice day." He then turned, got in his car, and drove away, with Jean still standing at the door, totally confused.

It took a moment for her to recover. But finally, she slowly walked to the couch, sat down, and opened the large envelope containing the documents. The first thing she noticed was a description of the loan on their property with a stamp that stated "Paid in Full." "What is this," she said out loud. "There must be some mistake."

She got on the phone to call the bank. When they answered and she told them who she was and that she was inquiring about their loan, the clerk who answered took a minute to check, then answered. "Mrs.

Peterson, your loan was handled personally by Mr. Dobson. He is the only one that can help you. Do you want me to transfer you?"

"Would you, please?"

She was put on hold for a couple of minutes before it was answered. "This is Mr. Dobson, may I help you?"

"This is Mrs. Peterson, and I think a mistake has been made. We have a mortgage loan on our home and have almost twenty years left on the contract. For some reason, I just received papers claiming the loan has been paid in full."

"Mrs. Peterson, let me check our records." Jean again waited on the phone as Mr. Dobson checked the records. He finally came back on the phone. "Mrs. Peterson, I am afraid I can't help you. Your mortgage loan was handled personally by my father. I am Adam Dobson. My father, Darrell, has retired. He is still president of the bank, but I am the manager. However, he has retained certain transactions in his personal care for some reason, and yours is one of those. Our records indicate your loan has been paid in full, but only he can explain the details."

"But how is that possible? We just made the regular payments.

"As I said, my father, even after his retirement, continued to handle a number of accounts. Only he can help you. I am sorry, but the records on your account are not available to anyone else here at the bank."

"How can I get in touch with your father? Do you have his number?"

"I'm sorry, but I can't give out private numbers. But if you will leave your name, number, and address, I will pass it on to him with your desire to talk to him."

"I would appreciate that." Then she left the information as requested with him.

"Is there anything else I can help you with?"

"No, thank you. You have been a great help."

They then said goodbye, and Jean hung up, still in bewilderment with even more questions. Why was their account personally handled by Darrell, and why doesn't the bank have access to the records on it? Jean wanted to call her husband but decided to wait until he got home. She did not want it on his mind while at work since he would be off in a couple of hours anyway.

When he got home, she immediately presented him with the envelope. "What is this?"

"Just open it."

When he did, his response was similar to Jean's. "I don't understand. Have you called the bank?"

"That was the first thing I did. Apparently, Darrell Dobson, who approved and signed the mortgage with us, has retired. His son, Adam Dobson, is now the bank manager and informed me his father is the only one with access to our loan records."

"But that does not make sense. Did you try to get in touch with Mr. Dobson senior?"

"They wouldn't give out his personal number. Adam took down our number and information on our loan and said he would forward it to his father with the request he contact us. All we can do is wait."

"This is crazy. We can't say anything about this to Liza. You know how she gets," he said.

Fortunately, Liza was at Roger's when Darrell called that evening. Jean answered the phone, and as soon as she found out it was Mr. Dobson, she motioned over Scott so they could both listen in.

"This is Darrell Dobson. My son informed me you were trying to get in touch with me. What can I do for you?"

"Mr. Dobson—"

"Darrell, please. I prefer being on a first-name basis."

"Well, since you called us at my request, you know we are the Petersons. We signed a thirty-year mortgage contract for our home about ten years ago. Today we received documents indicating the loan has been paid in full and we have a deed free and clear. There must be some mistake. Your son claimed the bank, which he is now president of, has no records regarding the loan and claims you personally oversaw it. We are at a loss. Could you please straighten things out?"

"There is nothing to straighten out, and there has been no mistake. And, yes, there were certain financial contracts I did handle myself and continue to handle on a personal basis. These accounts are of a personal nature where bank funds were not the main factor."

Now Scott spoke into the phone, "We are still confused."

"Your loan, along with a few others, was only partially backed by the bank. Remember when I approved yours how, at first, your request was denied? You didn't qualify. We finally worked things out to make an exception in your case. Your loan request, as far as the bank records, did not merit qualification. It was arranged, as I mentioned, through some creative measures I personally oversaw. Now that loan has been satisfied, and you now have a deed free and clear. There is no mistake. Any further information, I am not at liberty to provide. Now I can only congratulate you, and if there is nothing else, I wish you a good day."

At that, Jean and Scott together quietly, slowly said, "Thank you and goodbye." They both had been standing, and Jean slowly lowered herself on to the couch, still in shock. Scott just continued to stand still, holding the phone, not knowing what to say. He finally hung up the phone and joined his wife on the couch.

Jean finally spoke up, "What does this mean?"

"It means our home is free and clear, and we don't have any more house payments."

"But we owed over $200,000 on the loan. Things like this do not happen," Jean said.

Then they both looked at each other and, in unison, said, "Grandpa."

"But how did he know about our mortgage and who and what we owed. And where is getting all this money?" Scott said.

"This time our grandpa Santa has gone too far. We have to confront him. We have to do it together. Trying to confront him alone has never worked in the past. We have to face him with a united front. We have to talk some sense into him."

"Liza is over there right now," he said. "When do you want to go over there?"

Just then Liza walked in the door. "What's for dinner? I am starved. Nanny was in a bad mood, and Grandpa needed a little help." Then she noticed the table wasn't set, and her parents were just sitting together on the couch, something out of nature for them this time of day. Her father should be cleaning up and her mother preparing dinner. "What's going on?"

Her father spoke up, "Something has come up. Your mother and I have an errand to run. We'll be back in about an hour."

Jean, quick to pick up, ran to get her coat and purse. "I'm sorry, Liza, but we have to run. I started supper. It is in the oven. Can you be a good girl and watch it? It is a roast and will be done in about a half hour. Don't wait for us. We will eat when we get back."

Liza wanted to ask questions but just stood there as her parents rushed out the door.

When they got there, Roger was inside, and they didn't hesitate to let themselves in the back door. He was standing at the counter, apparently beginning to prepare his supper. Without turning, he said, "Did you forget something?" He then turned and saw it was not Liza as assumed. "Oh, it is you two? To what do I owe the privilege of both of your visit this time of evening?"

Scott spoke up first, "We came to discuss a little matter with you. We just found out the mortgage on our home has been paid off."

"That's good, congratulations. Why is it so urgent you have to inform me this time of night?"

Jean replied, "We thought you may know something about it." "That is good news, and I'm glad you got it paid off, but why come to me?"

"We didn't pay it off. We only made our regular payments and had almost twenty years left on the contract. It seems something or someone intervened."

"Maybe the mortgage company found some error and had to make a correction."

Jean, as usual, having a closer relationship with Roger, took over the debate, "Grandpa, don't act too innocent. You know very well how it happened. I don't know how you had the knowledge of it or how you managed to pay it off, but you have to stop paying off our bills. You have bought us two cars as well as who knows what else we don't know about. We know how you feel about Liza, and we accepted your generosity for her sake, but this is not for Liza. It is way too much. You can't possibly afford it. We can take care of our own bills." She was getting more and more agitated and was yelling, almost out of control.

Scott stepped in, "Calm down, honey. I know we are in agreement, but this is not the way to handle it. I'm sorry, Grandpa, but you know how much we love you, but that is why we want to protect and take care of you. This amount of money is unreasonable. You need to take care of yourself too. We can take care of our own debts."

Now, Roger, a little riled himself, adamantly gave his answer, "You are my family, and, as head of this family, it is not only my responsibility but my right to take care of it as I see fit. You don't know what I can or can't afford. Although it is none of your business, I can afford it. You know how I live, and that takes very little, and that is how I like it. I have no house payments, utilities are minimal, and food expenses are next to nothing. I have no car payments or any other debts. Feed for my animals is my biggest expense. That whole cost I can pay for with less than two weeks of retirement. So tell me, what do you suggest I spend my money on? I have told you before, helping others makes me happy, and that is all I have to live for. Do you just want me to lie down and die?"

Jean, at this time, became emotional and began drying her eyes and gave him a hug. "I'm sorry, Grandpa. Of course we don't want you to lie down and die. We love you and do want you to be happy. But you could use the money to take a nice vacation or do something you enjoy."

"I like the way I live. You, all of you, are what make me happy, and I wouldn't change a thing if I had all the money in the world. You are my world, can't you understand that?"

Jean was still in tears, in an embrace with Roger, and Scott stepped over to join in the hug. "We wouldn't want to change anything either."

They both finally realized there were no hidden motives behind their grandfather's actions. He did what he did for one reason. To make things easier for the people he loved, and trying to argue with him was futile. All you could do was smile and love him more. Then Jean started pulling him toward the door. "What are you doing?" he inquired.

"You are coming home with us, and I don't want any argument. We have a roast in the oven. You keep saying we are a family. Now it is time you acted like it." At that point, Scott put his arm around his other arm, and they escorted him out the door and into their car. He surprisingly didn't resist, and to the shock of Liza, the whole family enjoyed their first meal at the Peterson's.

After dinner, Liza insisted on driving Roger home. She knew something serious had taken place with her parents running out so suddenly and Roger ending up at their place for dinner. But she knew better than to get involved and didn't ask any questions. She just thanked him for finally joining them and hoping it could happen on a more regular basis.

Her parents, however, did discuss the matter during Liza's absence.

"That sneaky old man," commented Jean.

"What do you mean?"

"He did it again. He turned things around and made us forget why we came there. The issue of the mortgage was hardly mentioned. Come right down to it, he didn't really admit to it."

"Did you expect any other outcome? I think we accomplished a lot. We got him to finally come to our house. That's a big step. And besides, would you want him to be any other way?"

"You know, you're right. Come to think of it, there wasn't anything we could do about it anyway. It was done.

Chapter 25

Off to College

That dinner at the Peterson house was not to become a regular event. He did join them there, but it was a rare occasion. Most meals shared were at his home. He felt more comfortable there, and they could detect his nervousness while at their house. Besides, he insisted on helping in preparing meals at his place and felt completely out of place at theirs. By this time, they all felt as much at home at his place as they did at their own, so it just became more comfortable to share meals there.

One day as Jean was helping around the house at Roger's, she brought up the mortgage issue again. "I understand your incentive in paying off the mortgage, but we really could handle it. But now what are we going to do with our money? With no house payments, we will have more than we need."

"I know college expenses are high. You remember I attended college, and today's expenses are much higher than when I went. But a scholarship will not cover all the increased expenses of living away from home. She will need housing and food expenses, travel, and auto expenses. There will be books and other supplies. I know you wouldn't come to me each time she needed help, and there's no way to anticipate unexpected expenses. I don't want you to worry about how to pay for them. This way I know you can handle it without worry, and I don't want Liza to worry either. She needs to concentrate on her studies so she can come back a professional."

"I should have learned by now there is a logical reason for everything you do. Her getting a college degree is also a very important goal of Scott and I since neither of us were able to go. We are all on the same page there. Thank you."

"Why not?"

"Why not what?"

"It's not too late. You can go to college. You don't have to work now, and Liza will be off to school. Why not you? Or even Scott?"

"You have to be kidding. It is water under the bridge for us. As you said, we are happy the way things are now. Besides, who would take care of you?"

"I can take care of myself. What do you think I am, an invalid?"

She did know he needed help, especially with the animals, but she didn't want to push it. "I know, but you would miss me, and I would miss you."

"You know I won't dispute you on that. Come to think of it, maybe you better not go off to college."

She just hit him with a towel she was holding, leaned over, as he was sitting at the table, and gave him a big hug and smile. "You're impossible, you old goat." They just smiled at each other as they hugged each other.

The subject of the mortgage or any other financial aid from him never came up again.

As class president, Liza was obligated to speak at her graduation. Her grades also put her in the top five academically and one of the most, if not the most, popular students in the senior class. Again Roger was challenged to go out of his comfort zone. Liza reminded him he was the one to put her in the situation she was in. There was no way he was not going to attend her graduation. In fact, she insisted that if he didn't go, she wouldn't. Her parents were not going to let that happen. They were so proud of her, and seeing her up there on stage giving a speech as class president was the ultimate for them. With their help, their grandpa attended the ceremony. However, he stood in the back in the shadows. Andy was also there with his mother. Although Roger would never admit it, he had tears in his eyes as she gave her speech, especially when she referred to a special individual friend who took her under their wing soon after moving to Alderwood. Andy his mother had driven Roger to the school and took him home to avoid his exposure to others and allowed Liza to stay and celebrate and mingle with her classmates and their families.

Andy had somehow found out the about the money Roger had contributed to his college fund. But he never told anyone he knew. That knowledge greatly increased his respect and love for Roger. He recalled that night at Roger's, where he referred to Andy as his great-grandson, and Liza called him her brother. He knew Roger still didn't know he was the one who broke his window, but he realized it would not have made a difference to this old man. They didn't need a blood relationship. He was now accepted into an adoptive family he never had. That brought tears to his eyes as he gave a big smile. He had a sister and a grandpa—something he never had before.

Andy became more involved in the Peterson family as well as a special friend to Roger. He again went with Liza to tour the university to get her familiar with the campus now that she was going to be attending. He pointed out specific buildings and all other areas of interest. He even introduced her to the older couple he stayed with while attending the university and arranged for them to let her stay there with them. He vouched for her, and, with the relationship he had with them, they were eager to furnish housing for her. As it turned out, they were very reasonable in their rent, and she would be using the same bedroom and separate kitchen facilities as Andy used. Andy said in a kidding manner, "Take care of my room." And they both laughed. They felt comfortable with each other, and their relationship as brother and sister grew. He introduced her to everyone as a close relative to avoid any questions and suspicions.

Liza moved into the Wilsons', her new landlords, a couple of weeks before her first term began. As usual, Andy insisted on going with her to help move her in. He took his role as big brother very seriously not only because she was his connection to the individual whom he considered grandpa but because he really enjoyed her company.

Although he majored in political science and government and she was majoring in speech-language pathology and child psychology, Andy had become familiar with a lot of department heads at the college. He made it a point to look up the heads in the departments Liza was going to major in. On this visit, he made a point to introduce her to those he could make an appointment with. They were anxious to meet after what he had told about her. She was pleasantly surprised he went to so much trouble for her but excited to meet them and came away excited and anxious to get started. They were also impressed with her, and she was well on her way before the first day of school. They gave her a list of classes to take as well as useful information on preparing for the courses. She came away feeling comfortable knowing she would have the guidance available to help her obtain her degree.

Andy ended up spending two days with her, sleeping in another guest room of the Wilsons'. They were busy arranging meetings with teachers and department heads and familiarization with the campus and town. She would be required to do her own shopping and food preparation, so college was not the only thing she had to get familiar with.

Andy had intended to take the bus back home, but after the two days, Liza told him she had planned to return home for a week to say her goodbyes and spend time with everyone before she left for the semester. So they made the trip back together. Liza was so excited, talking about everyone she met, the advice they gave, and the campus, Andy hardly got a word in. The fact was even though it was Liza's car, he was glad he did the driving because she constantly used her hands as she talked, and felt uncomfortable with someone driving with their hands flying all over.

Everything was taken care of as far as enrollment and moving in. She had her class schedule and the keys to her new residence at the Wilsons'. That left her one week before returning to college, completely free to say her goodbyes to those she wished to. It was hard for her since she had never been away from home before. Her schoolmates were first on her list. Beth and Andy were next, and Andy promised to visit her off and on. He was committed to looking after his little sister, and besides, as an alumnus, he still had student friends and teachers he enjoyed visiting with. The Wilsons offered him to stay anytime his was in town. As an older couple, he helped around the place when he stayed there, and he became a part of the family. Saying goodbye to her animals, Roger, and her parents would be more difficult and something she was not looking forward to.

Knowing she had to leave early the next day, she could not put it off any longer. She first went into the barn. She wanted to squeeze Henrietta but knew even she would not like that. So she set her on her lap as usual, and they had their conversation. "I know you don't understand me, but I am going away for a while. Mama says she will visit and hold you. I want you to be nice." Henrietta looked up at her as if she did understand and clucked quietly. Their bond was strong, with their conversations sometimes emotional when Liza felt depressed. Henrietta seemed to, like most animals, assess her mood and offered what comfort she could. Liza stroked her soft feathers and eventually lifted her up to give her a kiss. Then she sat her down and walked out of the barn.

It was hard saying goodbye to her chicken, but she knew the next would be even harder. She entered Nanny's corral as she was bleating, which she had been since Liza entered the property. Liza didn't have to go to Nanny. She was waiting for her at the gate with anticipation. Nanny wanted to play, as usual, but Liza grabbed her around the neck and, with her head against her, said her goodbye. "I can't play today. I only came to tell you I am going away for a while. I'll be back, but I want you to be good while I am gone. Be nice to Grandpa. He will need you while I'm gone. And stop butting Mama when she tries to milk you." She had tears in her eyes as she finally let go. "I love you, Nanny. Be good, I'll see you when I get back." Then she closed the gate and headed to the porch where Roger was waiting for her.

She knew this was going to be hard. She didn't know how she could get through it. "Grandpa," she said through tears, "I'm going to miss you. I love you so much. I don't know what I'll do without you.

You have made everything possible for me." She continued to hold him in a big bear hug as they sat together on the swing.

"No, little princess, you did everything for me. You are a strong young woman now, and you don't need me. You are who you are because of your hard work and determination. You are destined to do wonderful things and help many people who need you."

"Grandpa, you are the one who showed me how important it is to help others and the joy it brings. And I do need you."

He then gently pushed her away and looked her in the eyes. "I will always be with you in here." And he put his hand to her heart. "And you will always be here." And he placed his hand over his heart.

Liza smiled through her tears and gave him another hug. "All right," he said. "You'll never get to school this way, and your parents will be wanting to give you a proper send-off." He then got up, with her hanging on, and led he to her car. He opened the door for her and made sure she got in safely. Liza was too distraught to say anything, so they just waved at each other as she drove out the driveway. Roger slowly walked back to his house with mixed emotions. College for Liza was a main goal for them, but parting was hard, and his vision was blurred with the water he could not hold back. He had always tried to show the heart of a lion, but he now felt like a little kitten.

When she arrived home, she was still sobbing, and both her parents gave her a group hug. "I know dear," her mother said. "It is hard. But we knew this time would come. You have worked so hard for this. You are a young woman now, no longer a child. You have to accept the changes and keep moving forward."

"Grandpa told me the same thing. He said I was destined to help others and college is a step I have to take. But that doesn't make it any easier."

Her mother finally said, "It is getting late. You have had a long day, and you have to get up early tomorrow. Why don't you get ready for bed? I'll fix you something to eat and bring it to you so you can have some time alone."

After Liza left to get cleaned up in the bathroom, her parents joined each other in the kitchen, where Jean began preparing something to eat. They hadn't eaten yet either, but she wanted to fix something quick for Liza, and they would eat leftovers. She began to tear up. "We are losing our little girl. What are we going to do?"

"We aren't losing her," Scott replied. "She is only going to school just a few hours away. She will be back for visits, and when she graduates, she will come back home. She is not a little girl anymore. She is a young lady. A young lady I am proud to say is my daughter. She is growing up, and we have to grow with her. Change is a part life we can't stop. We will be better off embracing it and not fighting it."

"I know, but…why do you always have to be the strong one? What would I do without you?'

"I hope you never have to find out. But to make you feel better, inside I am mush."

Jean just laughed and gave him a big hug and a kiss.

The next morning was "D-Day" for Liza. Nothing was said until they reached the door and reality set in. "Are you sure you have everything?" asked her mother.

"Yes, Mama, you helped me pack."

"Drive careful, and give us a call as soon as you get there," her father said.

But as Liza got to her car with parents in tow and her father holding the car door open, things came to a standstill. She couldn't let go of her parents as they hugged, kissed, and shed tears. "Well," her father finally said, "let's break this up. You have a long drive ahead of you. I don't want you driving in the dark."

"Dad, I have made this trip five times already, twice by myself. I think I will be all right. Take care of Grandpa. He's not as strong as he pretends to be."

"Go," her father said. "Get out of here. We'll take care of Grandpa and Nanny and the chickens. Just get out of here."

With that, she backed out of the driveway, and they all waved goodbye, leaving her mother standing there in tears.

Chapter 26

Relations Develop

Liza did call every night as promised, at least in the beginning. Soon, however, she reverted to calling about every third night. With the responsibility of preparing her own meals, washing clothes, and keeping up her apartment along with her studies, she found free time very limited. With all the new responsibilities, homesickness was a thing of the past most of the time. Time seemed to fly by, and her first trip home a month later, she was anxious to share her activities at school. She was overjoyed to see everyone again, but this time there were smiles with hugs instead of tears. With only a three-day break, she had to ration out her time and keep a tight schedule. Grandpa and her animals was a priority, and a whole day was devoted to them. Nanny and Henrietta obviously missed her as she did them, but Grandpa wanted to know everything. He wanted to know about every class she was taking and their professors. He wanted to know how she was getting along with her landlords and if she had a boyfriend. Nothing was out-of-bounds with him.

One day, she set aside to visit other friends and the Christiansons. The last day would be devoted to her parents, as that day, she would be returning to school. The farewells this time were less emotional. In fact, Liza seemed anxious to get back to school. They could tell she had adjusted very well to her independence.

There were other adjustments taking place at home. Jean, who had devoted her whole life to Liza, now had to channel her efforts in another direction. Her desire to have a large family and then finding out after giving birth to Liza that she no longer could have children had devastated her. Doubling her efforts to take care of her daughter's needs became an obsession. Her whole being was devoted to her, and now she felt empty.

Even though Scott and Jean were spending more and more time at Roger's, he was also showing signs of depression without Liza around. Now that their home was paid off, Jean's extra income was no longer needed, and she only filled in when they really needed her. That left her more time to spend at Roger's. In fact, she spent almost every day there, and Scott soon met them there after work. That left a lot of time for Jean and Roger to talk and get to know each other better. After the daily chores were accomplished, and they felt like taking a rest, Jean would relax on the recliner in the living room, and Roger would lie down on his little bed. They would talk while relaxing, and oftentimes, one or the other, or both, would fall asleep.

On one of these rest periods, Jean exposed pains she had lived with. "You know I wanted a large family, but circumstances changed our plans."

"Yes, I knew your desire of a larger family. I'm sorry, but you have a lovely daughter."

"Yes, she is a godsend, but it was not always so. I feel it is time I let someone in. I can see you miss Liza as much as I do. She has been my life. Finding I could not bear any more children after Liza was born devastated me. I became very depressed and didn't want anything to do with her. In fact, I didn't want to live. But I have a wonderful husband who took care of not only me but Liza as well. I guess his experience taking care of his grandmother prepared him. It took about two months for me to come out of it. But when I did, I became overprotective of Liza. She was everything to me, and, to be honest, my relationship with Scott suffered. As I said, he was, and is, an angel. With his patience, I finally came down to earth and faced reality. When Liza started stuttering, I didn't know how to handle it, but he again was able to calm me down and face it head-on. She has become the center of my life, and without her here, I'm scared."

"You didn't have to tell me this. But since you have, I completely understand. I guess I look at Liza in the same way. She has saved me as well. I have always said she was special, and your story proves it. But we aren't losing her. She will be back, and we have each other. She has made us both strong enough to face those goblins of the past."

There were other conversations, most on a more pleasant nature. In fact, they liked to tease and make fun of each other and, at times, ended up with pillows flying across the room. Previous encounters, mostly regarding financial issues, showed Roger as taking charge, showing the alpha in his nature. As their relationship developed, Jean became the mother hen. Roger became her child she felt she had to protect. Their disagreements, in some cases outright arguments, ended with him giving in to her. In some cases, he had no choice. She took over the care of his house and treated him like a child at times. But it was all good-naturedly, and they usually ended up in each other's arms, laughing. With the chickens, Nanny, and Roger, she got her family, and Roger got his family.

Scott was not left out. He and Roger spent hours gathering and preparing wood to be worked into the finished products they put together in the workshop. Scott learned not only the use of small tools in the workshop but the larger power tools in the outer shop. Carpentry became a necessity on the small farm, and he became familiar with the use of the tools of that trade. He found he liked working with his hands and using his imagination and figuring things out on his own. Creativity was, he found, very rewarding. He and Roger became a team, and together they were able to accomplish things that, alone, would be almost impossible to do.

Eventually, almost all evening meals took place at Roger's.

With the insistence of Jean, it was decided sleeping in the living room was no longer a suitable situation for their grandpa. It was decided the shop would be transformed to its original purpose, a bedroom. To do that, the inner shop had to be moved to the larger shop and storeroom. And that had to be moved to the open garage that would be enclosed and made into a outer storage shop. The pickup would be moved into the barn, where the stalls on one side would be transformed into a garage. There was already a connecting door between the small inner shop to the outer shop, but it was determined a door from the to-be bedroom was needed into the bathroom directly. Plans were drawn up for the changes despite Roger's objections. Jean was the head of this house now, and when she gave him the stink eye, he had to relent.

Although it sounded like a lot of work, the only real structural changes was the door from the bedroom into the bathroom. And this became a little tricky. It was a small bathroom with a shower, small counter with a sink, toilet, and the water heater. They had to move the counter with the sink a couple of feet toward the water heater.

This gave them just enough room against the outside wall to install a doorway. Everything else was just a matter of moving and building shelves and moving things around. There was already a door from the porch into the outside shop where the larger tools were kept and used. The bedroom now ended up having three doorways—one to the kitchen, one to the bathroom, and one to what would become his shop. The shop also had three doorways—one to the bedroom, one out to the porch, and one, with one step down, into the large tool shop and wood storage room, which was previously the garage.

The garage had a cement floor that was raised above ground level to avoid rain and snow from coming in. It now would be used for wood storage and for the larger tools like table saw and bank saw. It was just a matter of installing a pair of hinged swinging doors on the front. With all three working together, the house remodeling was accomplished within a few weeks. Most of the work was just a matter of moving tools and fixtures, such as benches, cabinets, and shelves from one room to the next.

Jean, as expected, became foreman and supervisor, but she had to conform to Roger's demands that everything be put back as it was in the previous room. She did, however, put the woman's touch to things and did her share of the work when she could. When it was finished, they all stood back in pride. "A family that works together stays together," Roger said, and they all laughed.

Since there were no changes to the outside and no major structural changes inside, the status as a historical site was maintained. The garage door addition had no effect, and any modifications made in the barn would not affect the status either. The barn was fairly small with a small loft. The pen for the chickens took up the left side. The right side still had stalls, but they took them out so they could drive the pickup all the way to the back of the barn. They enclosed it and again put hinged doors to close it up. They left space between the chicken pen and garage to leave a walkway to the back where there was a door to the outside of the barn to allow access to the back of the property. Just inside the front door of the barn, to the right in the first stall was a fruit cellar with a trapdoor. This was there when Roger moved in, and doubled as a storm cellar, even though they never had any severe storms in the area.

Jean didn't participate in the barn remodeling, and even when it was done, the pickup was seldom parked in the new garage inside. They usually parked it just inside the barn or left it outside. They just wanted someplace for it when the weather was bad during the winter and yet would stay somewhat clean from the dust that was common inside a barn.

They didn't use the pickup very often, but they still used it to pick up feed and hay as well as building material. Roger also used it to take Nanny to her original owner to breed. They found it came in handy for unexpected items and was a fixture of the property and made the place appear to be a real farm.

During this construction period, the bonding continued. There was no more "Roger" or "Roger's place." It became "Grandpa" and "our place." Jean and Scott now felt as if they belonged there and they had two homes. And Grandpa, Jean insisted, was not going to sleep in that tiny cot he called a bed anymore. "Get that thing out of here," she told her husband. "You can pick it up when you next collect the trash."

"So am I supposed to sleep on the floor?" Roger inquired.

"Of course not, we are going to take the pickup and go buy you a new full-size bed. Are you going to come along, or are you willing to accept what we pick out?"

"But I don't need a new bed."

"You most definitely do! That thing is falling apart and so full of lice it moves on its own. You are not going to move into that new bedroom we all worked so hard to fix up for you with that piece of garbage. Now are you going to come with us or not?"

Scott turned his back to them, with his hand covering his mouth. He was having a hard time keeping from bursting out in laughter.

"Go ahead without me. I guess I'll have to something to sleep on since you are throwing away my bed."

Then Jean walked over to him and gave him a kiss and a hug. "I love you, you old goat. We'll have to buy new linen to fit as well. I think we'll get something in pink."

This time, Scott couldn't hold it back and burst out laughing. Roger put his hands to his hips and gave her a dirty look that ended up into a smile. "Get out of here, bossy, before I take a broom to you."

When Jean and Scott were in the truck, he commented, "You shouldn't tease him so much. You were actually cruel."

"He loves it. It makes him feel alive. It's not just one-sided. We banter back and forth, but we both know it is all in fun. And making up just brings us closer. Deep inside, we both know we would do anything for each other, and the little bickering just shows we care."

"You know anyone seeing you two together would think you were really related and grew up together."

"He is my grandpa! And we both feel we should have grown up together. At least I wish we had. I needed a grandpa, and now that I have one, I'm going to take of advantage of it. Now let's get that bed."

"You weren't serious about pink, were you?"

"Of course not, I just wanted to twist the knife."

"You know, you really are evil."

They ended up getting him a nice double bed that they both tested out and felt was very comfortable. They also purchased two sets of linen with pillows that were white, not pink. When they got home and set up the bed and made it up, Roger just smiled, said "thank you," and gave them each a hug.

Chapter 27

A Visit Home

Time seemed to fly by for Liza. She immersed herself in her studies. She took not only the mandatory courses but also anything she felt could enhance her knowledge in her field of study. She was constantly consulting with her department head for advice and suggestions as to which courses to take and what order to take them. Her enthusiasm led to suggested readings, by her instructors, of publications outside the required ones for her classes.

She did call home on a regular basis but seldom found loneliness to be an issue. She was taking a full load plus, and her class schedule was busy. Some days, she had classes from eight in the morning to six in the evening with few breaks between. The assignments and reports, along with constant studying, lasted late into the evening. She found herself studying while eating, doing food preparation, and washing clothes. She often fell asleep with a book in her hand.

Her visits home became less frequent, facilitating the visits by Andy. Despite her calls, or maybe because of them, her parents and Roger became worried about her. Andy would visit to check up on her and make sure she took time to relax. He would usually take her to a restaurant he liked while there. She would object, saying she didn't have time, but he, along with support from the Wilsons, would prevail. Her landlords expressed to Andy their concern for Liza's hectic schedule. They were impressed with her devotion but, being in a college town and previously housing students, knew the danger of emotional burnout.

He drove up one Friday to visit her and talked to the Wilsons before she returned from her classes.

When she returned home, she noticed Andy's car in the driveway. It was not that that much of a surprise since he did visit once in a while. But when she entered the door, he was standing there. "Grab what you need, I'm taking you home."

"I can't, I have too much to do and assignments to work on."

"Monday is a holiday. You have a three-day weekend. You can work on your assignments and study at home."

"But I have clothes to wash and cleaning to do."

"Stop making excuses. You can bring your dirty clothes, and they can be done there. Now go get what you need. It is getting late, and I would like to be back before it gets too late. It is going to be late as it is. I'll make sure you're back Monday before it gets too late."

Mrs. Wilson, who had been listening from the living room, suddenly appeared. "Young lady, Andy has made this long trip because he is concerned for your well-being, and so are we. You do as he says. I will clean your apartment and wash your clothes. You need a break. I don't want to hear any more if, ands, or buts. Now get out of here."

"You heard her. Don't forget, I lived here for four years, and Mrs. Wilson can be pretty forceful."

"This isn't fair! You are ganging up on me."

Mrs. Wilson just looked at her with her head at a tilt. "Liza."

"Okay, but I will take and do my own laundry."

Andy followed her downstairs to help her and make sure she didn't dawdle or change her mind. Her apartment was a mess, but he knew it would be clean when she got back. As she gathered her dirty clothes and packed them clean, Andy asked which books and other material she wanted to take along, and he gathered it up. "You don't need your whole wardrobe. I'm sure you have more at home. Now let's go."

He ended up throwing her books and other things in the suitcase with her clean clothes as she stuffed the dirty ones in a large laundry bag. He carried the suitcase, and she carried the bag of clothes up the stairs, and the Wilsons gave both of them a hug and said goodbye as they walked out the door. Liza, still upset, remained quiet.

Once in the car, Andy just let her pout for a while. Once out of town, he broke the silence, "Liza, we are all worried about you. Your parents and everyone at home want to see you. You haven't been home for over two months. You're pushing yourself too hard. They all miss you, and I miss my little sister."

She looked over at him finally, with a smile. She took his hand in hers. "I know, but there is so much to do and learn. I don't have the time."

"You do have the time. You forget I was in college too, and I have seen dedicated students burn out. Some couldn't handle it and left, others ended up unable to concentrate and could not complete assignments or even follow lectures. Sleep deprivation and the sheer pressure ended up with some ending up under doctor's care and having to leave school. I don't want that happening to you. You are going to be a great therapist, but only if you can get your degree."

Before he finished, Liza was leaning against him, sound asleep. He just smiled and put his arm around her. By the time she woke up, it was getting dark, and they were only an hour from home.

As she stirred and wiped her eyes, Andy said, "Good morning, or should I say good evening? Did you have a good nap? We'll be home pretty soon. There is some water, snacks, and sandwiches in the back seat if you are thirsty or hungry. I know you haven't had anything to eat since leaving for classes this morning, but I didn't want to wake you."

She smiled at him. "How long have I been asleep?"

"About four and a half hours. You must have been exhausted."

"Apparently I was, but didn't realize how much. And, yes, I am famished." She then reached back into the back and grabbed some water and a sandwich. "Do you want one? There seem to be plenty." "No, thank you. I just have to work out the numbness in my arm and side."

She just looked at him with a smile and slapped him on his numb arm, and they both laughed. The rest of the trip was spent in mostly silence as Liza devoured another sandwich and some snacks.

When they pulled up into the Peterson driveway, Liza swung open the car door and ran to her parents with her arms open. They had been waiting for her, and as soon as the car entered the driveway, they were out the front door and waiting for her on the front porch. Then the water fountains began as they gave a big group hug. Her busy schedule kept her from thinking about missing everyone, but it all came back in earnest now. Andy, for his part, had grabbed the suitcase and laundry bag and was headed up the walk. Scott noticed him and rushed to help. "Here, let me help." And he grabbed the suitcase from him. He led Andy into the house with their burdens as Liza and her mom continued their embrace. They never bothered to close the door as they rushed out to greet their daughter. As the men entered the house, the women finally followed them with their arms around each other.

"Thank you, my son," Scott said. "We really appreciate you doing this for us. Her mother was at wit's end when she received the call from the Wilsons. You don't know how much we appreciate your kindness and concern. By the way, just put those down, we'll take care of them. It has been a long day for you. I'm sure your mother is worried, and you need something to eat and get to bed. You have driven over five hundred miles almost without a rest. You have to be exhausted. You are a godsend to us. Again, thanks."

They gave each other a hug, and Andy said. "You don't have to thank me. I miss my little sister too, and I will always be there for her and you. Good evening." He then turned, walked to his car, and drove away.

Jean, who had been emotionally involved in welcoming her daughter home, finally turned to her husband. "Where is Andy going? I didn't get a chance to thank him or even say hi?"

"It's okay," her husband said. "I thanked him for both of us. He needed to get home. It has been a long drive for him." He had gained a greater respect and appreciation for the man who considered himself a big brother to his daughter. He realized just how close their relationship had grown, and it made him smile.

They visited late into the night. It only reminded her how much she missed everyone at home. Even though she slept a good portion of the trip home in the car, once she hit her own bed at home, she was out like a rock.

The next morning, she woke up rested and relaxed for the first time in weeks and anxious to go to Grandpa's. As she was running around and heading for the door, her mother stopped her. "Hold on, young lady. You aren't going anywhere until you have something to eat. As soon as we all have something, we will all take the car and go to the farm together."

"The farm? I thought it was still referred to as Grandpa's?"

"There have been a few changes since you have been gone." Her father exclaimed. Upon the insistence of Grandfather, we now have two residences. His place is now our farm, and this is our home. You may be surprised at some of the changes we made there. We haven't mentioned it to you because we wanted you to be surprised and also because we wanted to talk about what was happening with you."

"What kind of changes?"

"Just finish your breakfast, and you can see for yourself when we get there." Liza started to inhale her food. "Slow down, you'll make yourself sick. You have to wait for your father and I anyway."

"I can walk."

"You're not going to walk," her father said. "We are still your parents, and we know what is best for you. Besides, we are not going to let you out of our sight. Now eat slowly."

As soon as they were finished, Liza wasted no time clearing the table and putting the dishes in the dishwasher.

"All right, everyone get your jackets on, and get in the car. It is a little chilly out."

As soon as they got there, Liza rushed to Nanny, who, which was out of character for her, was very quiet. However, as soon as Liza got to the gate, Nanny started her normal bleating in earnest. She opened the gate and they rushed to each other and Liza put her arms around her neck and they put their heads together. "I missed you so much," she said as Nanny continued bleating.

Hearing the commotion, Grandpa came out the back door with his walking stick. "She missed you, you know. She has been depressed, and no matter how much we tried, she would not play with anyone, and her milk production is minimal. She spends most of her time laying down, and it's been hard to even get her to eat."

"Grandpa!" she yelled. She then pulled herself away from her embrace and ran to him. "I missed you so much." And she gave him a big hug.

"Then why have you stayed away so long? Nanny and I, and even Henrietta, have missed you. Your mother has been talking to Henrietta, so I think she understands, but I know she will also be happy to see you. Let's go talk to her." At that he led her to the barn with his arm around her waist and his walking stick in the other hand. When they opened the pen, Liza ran to Henrietta and picked her up and sat down on the chair kept there and started to talk to her. Henrietta was getting older and slower, but it was obvious she recognized Liza as she looked up at her. Roger stood there, leaning against a barn support pillar with a smile as they talked to each other as if nothing had changed. Her parents walked into the barn and, with their arms around each other's waist, stood there smiling as they watched their little girl happy and back where she belonged.

Then Liza noticed the changes to the inside of the barn. The pickup was parked outside when she entered, and at that time, Henrietta was her only interest. "What did you do to the barn?" she inquired.

"We made a few modifications so we could park the truck in here," her father offered.

"What's the matter with the garage?"

"Well, that is part of some of the changes we told you about," said her mother. "Would you like to see the rest? You can come out and spend more time with Henrietta and Nanny later." With that Liza realized Nanny was continuing to bleat but agreed to follow them to the house to be shown the rest of the changes.

As they were walking, she noticed the door on the used-to-be garage, but it didn't register as anything significant. She observed no other changes from the outside and wondered what the changes were. As she entered the kitchen, she could see into the living room. "What happened to Grandpa's bed?"

Roger, tired from the walk and standing, sat down at the table without saying a word, allowing the tour to be done by Scott and Jean. It was all their idea, and they had done most of the work, so they should have the privilege of showcasing their labors. Without a word, Jean opened the door to the now bedroom. "You have a bedroom, Grandpa, and a real bed."

He just smiled and said, "And it is not pink." Her parents, along with Grandpa, all laughed.

"What is so funny?" she said.

"We'll fill you in later," her father answered. "Would you like to see the rest of the house?

Without any more conversation, they showed the bathroom with the adjoining door to the bedroom and then led her from room to room through the inside doors and into what used to be the garage. "How do you like it?" her mother asked when they all joined Grandpa in the kitchen.

The only thing she could say was "Grandpa has a bedroom and a real full-size bed, with a private door to the bathroom."

"It was your mother's idea," Roger said. "And they did most of the work. I said it wasn't necessary, but I admit I like the new bed, especially since it doesn't have pink bedding." Then all but Liza laughed again.

"What is this story with pink?" Liza asked again.

Then they explained to her the story, and they all had a good laugh. They all had a good visit, with her grandpa asking her all kinds of questions. As usual, he wanted to know everything, and the questioning went on for hours. Her parents took time to feed and do other necessary duties in the care of the animals. Roger took that time alone with Liza to discuss something serious. "You know Nanny is getting along. Her decreased milk production is not only due to her missing you."

"I know you have to breed ever so often so she has a kid so she can continue to give milk. We have done it before."

"She is not going to have any more kids. I have another nanny coming as soon as she can be separated from her kid so I will have a milk producer."

"What are you saying? You're going to replace Nanny?" she said, noticeably upset.

"No, Liza, settle down. Nanny is your goat, and we will never get rid of, or replace, her. We will just have two goats until her time comes."

"You mean until she dies. We have had these discussions before about the circle of life. I'm not a child. I'm under no illusion. All life comes to an end sooner or later. As a future therapist, that is an issue I will probably have to handle with clients. I can handle it. How long do you think she has?"

"It's hard to say. But I'd say two to three years, maybe five at the most. She has been a good companion. It will be hard to see her go."

"I know we will both miss her. It's really going to be especially hard for me. She was my first friend after moving here. She has been my anchor. Do Mom and Dad know?"

"No, but your father and I will go together to pick up the new nanny, and I'll let him know then. He can break it to your mom. You can name her, and she can be yours like Nanny."

"No, there will never be another Nanny for me. She will always be with me in here." And she placed her hand to her heart.

The rest of her visit was somewhat in a somber mood. Although she did visit her other friends and school teachers she felt close to, she spent a lot of the rest of her visit home at the farm with Nanny and Henrietta. Even though her parents thought it a little excessive, they knew of the close connection they had and didn't think too much of it.

When the time came to return to school, Andy was there early Monday to pick her up as promised. Her departure was again filled with hugs and kisses, but not as hard as before. She was growing up, and it turned out the departure the night before at the farm was the hardest. The trip back was uneventful and, for the most part, silent. No more sleeping against Andy. He let her go over her thoughts in silence, sensing she was in no mood to talk. When he dropped her off, now with all clean clothes which her mother had cleaned, he didn't even go inside. They just gave each other a hug, and she gave him a kiss on the cheek. She told him "thank you" and walked into the house. Andy stood there a minute, then got into the car and drove home.

Chapter 28

Passing of a Friend

During her summer break between semesters, Liza stayed at the university. She had taken on a voluntary position at the university hospital, working in the children's ward. She would help and observe as doctors dealt with those with emotional issues. Although she could not qualify as an intern, she was allowed to observe, and they always welcomed any volunteers. Most of the time, she just helped clean up, changed beds, served meals, and did what she could to make patients comfortable. The doctors and nurses, however, were free with advice and information that would help in her studies. Some of the doctors were actually instructors at the university in advanced courses she would be taking. She was all in when it came to her studies and determined to do all she could to be a well-rounded psychologist and speech therapist.

A couple of weeks before her first semester of her second year was to begin, she got a call from her mother that brought her to her knees. Henrietta had passed away. There was no question in her mind. There was to be a funeral, and Liza was going to be there to conduct it. It was her pet and her decision and responsibility.

Since her duties at the hospital were voluntary, her presence was not mandatory, and she immediately called them to let them know she would not be able to help for the next two weeks. She was packed and on her way within an hour, filling in the Wilsons on her sudden change of plans and when she planned to be back.

Her trip home was filled with sorrow and tears and fortunate in the fact she didn't get stopped for speeding. She didn't bother stopping at her parents' house but instead went directly to the farm, where she was sure they would all be there since it was still early afternoon. She sped into the driveway and was out of the car and at the back porch before anyone knew she was there. They were all in the house, waiting for her to arrive. Roger and Scott had placed the chicken in a wooden box they had made for her.

Liza ran in. "Where is she?"

"Your father and I made a casket for her and placed her in it. It is in the barn," her adopted grandfather said.

"I want to see her."

"A dead chicken, Liza, is not a pretty sight. It's better to remember her as she was. We nailed it shut. We were just waiting for you to arrive so you could oversee her burial and services. We also made a cross with her name on it to make the site. We can place her in the woods behind. You can pick out the site."

"But I want to see her!"

"Liza," her mother said, "I saw her, and Grandpa is right. You don't want to see her the way she looks now. She died in the night, and one night can do a lot to a dead chicken."

With that, Liza wept as she was embraced in her mother's arms. Roger gave Scott a nod of the head, and he went out to the barn to collect the box with Henrietta. Since Roger had trouble getting around now, Scott, or Jean, automatically took over most activities that required walking. Jean and Roger, with his walking stick and arm around Liza's shoulder for support, walked Liza between them out the back door. Her dad was on his way back from the barn, and as they all headed for the woods, her father stopped by the toolshed to get a shovel. Her father also had the cross, which he handed to Liza. They continued into the woods behind the fruit trees until they found a spot under a large alder tree that Liza selected.

Scott dug the hole and placed the cross at the site. There was a short simple ceremony. Liza wasn't the only one who would miss Henrietta and was saddened by her passing. Jean had spent a lot of time holding and talking to her, especially after Liza was gone and she felt lonely. Roger had been holding and talking to her before Liza came along. Even Scott had sat and held her on occasion.

The grave was soon covered, and then Liza said, "I love you, Henrietta, and I will always remember you. Goodbye."

They all then stood there with their heads bowed, but Liza lingered as Jean and Scott walked back to the house with their grandfather between them. They knew Liza would like to spend some alone time with her pet. They walked back to the house in silence and remained that way as they sat at the kitchen table.

Liza remained another half hour on her knees, still in tears and expressing her devotion for her special friend. When she finally returned, she could hear Nanny bleating for her. In fact, she had been bleating from the time she drove up. But everyone was so involved in the task at hand that they didn't pay attention to her. Now Liza not only noticed. She ran to the gate, opened it, and gave Nanny a big hug as she met her there. The tears came again as her emotions took over. Then she became aware of another animal present. It had not approached her but was standing quietly nearby, looking at them. Liza then remembered that, on a previous visit, Grandpa had told her he was getting another goat, but she had forgotten all about it. She now had something new introduced to her life, but at this time, she was not up to dealing with it.

After holding and talking to Nanny for a while, she returned to the house where the rest of her family were patiently waiting. She sat down at the table where everyone sat silently. She then spoke up, "When did you get the other goat, Grandpa?"

"We have had her for about a month now. I mentioned it to you on your last visit."

"I remember, but it was just unusual to find another goat in Nanny's pen. Have you named her yet?"

"We thought we would leave that up to you. Nanny is still the queen of the barnyard even though we do not milk her anymore. We just call the new goat, goat, and she is a good milk producer. But Nanny lets her know who is in charge. We were waiting for you to name her. If you like, she can be yours."

"I have Nanny, and that is the only animal I want. You can name her."

"Her mother spoke up, "She still needs love, Liza. It's not her fault she is the second goat. You could show her a little attention at least."

"I'm not going to stay here, so there is no reason for me to get to know her or get attached. Nanny is all I need. I think I'll go home."

"Okay," her father said. "I guess it is time we all went home."

"No, I want to walk. I need time to be alone and work things out in my mind. I need to practice what, as a psychologist, I will be advising others to do. I'll be all right. You stay and help out here. Grandpa needs you, and I know there are things to take care of."

As she walked out the door, the others looked at each other and gave a shrug. Her parents stayed another two hours to help out on the farm but also to give her the alone time she requested. When they did arrive home, she was on the couch, reading a book. "What are you reading?" her mother inquired.

"It's a book I borrowed from one of my instructors on handling disturbed children facing stressful situations. I think it is quite appropriate at this time."

He father went over and sat down by her. "And how are you feeling right now?"

"You know, I am feeling much better. I realized I have been acting childish. I have to start acting like an adult, a professional adult. Grandpa has been exposing me to and teaching me about the cycle of life for years. He has been preparing me for things like this. It is a part of life. And I handled it like a child. He didn't have to get a degree or go to college to teach me those lessons, and I completely didn't take it seriously. If I don't take my studies any more serious than I did his lessons, I am not going to be a success in my profession. This has been a wake-up call for me."

"But how are you feeling?"

"I am dealing with it. These situations bring on sadness and depression, but you can't let them affect your life going on, and I have to pick myself up and go on. I think we should name the new goat Annie. Like little orphan Annie."

Jean and Scott just looked at each other and smiled. She was going to be fine. Their little girl was growing up fast. The rest of her vacation at home was spent mostly at the farm. She visited friends, but along with helping out, she got to know Annie, and the three of them became good playmates. Nanny was still her goat, and although she had no intention of adopting Annie, the name her parents decided to name the new goat after Liza left, it didn't mean they could not become good friends.

Time flew by, and she had returned for the first semester of her junior year. She was also anxious to get back to her volunteer service at the hospital, now with a new perspective on emotional complications. Grandpa's method of practical experience for learning, along with her experience, was a great asset, and along with the formal education, she now felt better prepared to become the best psychologist possible.

Chapter 29

A Major Loss

Liza's dedication to her studies put her at the top of the class in her department. Instructors took notice and took her under their personal guidance. She still had required general studies classes to complete for a degree, but her curriculum was devoted to courses in her field of study. They included courses in child psychology and development, every psychology course she could squeeze in, as well as those studies available in the field of stuttering. She continued to volunteer at the hospital psychiatric ward. Her dedication and enthusiasm gained her scholarships from the department and hospital college funds. You could say she became a very successful student as well as popular not only in her department but the professors throughout the school.

Her trips home were limited, but she made the effort to visit on a more regular basis. She realized the breaks helped ground her and were needed to recharge her. On these visits, her studies were set aside. She spent the time visiting friends, working on the farm, and getting better acquainted with Annie. During this year, Andy had been elected to the city council and became engaged. Liza made a point of spending time with them, and they became a close threesome. They all enjoyed each other's company, and there was no jealousy on Andy's fiancée because he had introduced Liza as his little sister and treated her as such. Arial, his fiancée, was informed of their true relationship and their story, but it only added to their close relationship.

Everything was going along smoothly when she again got a call that stopped her in her tracks. She just stood there, holding the phone in silence. Nanny had passed away. She had lost her two best friends and pets in the same year. This time it did not come at a good time. It was at the end of the second semester of the year, and she was in the middle of finals.

She was on the phone with her father. "Liza, you take care of your finals. Your education is paramount, and we all know how important your finals are. Concentrate on them. You said you have only a week to go. We will take care of things here. We can hold her in refrigeration until you can make it home. We will wait until then to do anything."

"But, Dad, I have a couple of days before tests begin. I can come down for a day for the funeral and come back for the tests."

"No, you need the time to study and keep your mind on things there. As I said, we can handle things here and won't do anything until you get here. Now would you please let me talk to Mrs. Wilson for a minute?"

She wasn't sure why her father wanted to talk to Mrs. Wilson, but assumed it was regarding the rent, which her parents took care of. When Liza found Mrs. Wilson, she handed her the phone. "Yes, can I help you?"

"Clara, this is Scott." Over the years, they had come to a first-name basis. "An issue has come up that I think you should be aware of, and I would like your help. I'm sure you know of Nanny, Liza's pet goat?"

"Yes, Liza mentions her often. They seem to have a close relationship."

"She had died."

"Oh no, that is going to be very upsetting for Liza."

"That is the reason I am asking for your help. You and your husband have been outstanding hosts, and we appreciate everything you have done for her. She needs some emotional support at this time, but she has finals coming up. It is essential she concentrate on those. She feels obligated to be here for the funeral and wants to come home now and go back for the tests. We are insisting on her staying until the tests are complete. We know she needs to study for them, and she couldn't if she were to come home. Could you see that she sticks to her studies and do what you can to relieve her of any pressure? I know you have a calming influence, and she could use your understanding and support at this time."

"Of course, I understand. We will do what we can. We know how emotional and driven she is. She has been able to handle things more calmly since her chicken died, but this is going to be a terrible shock to her. Don't worry, she has become like a daughter to us, and we will take care of her."

"Thank you, you don't know how much we appreciate it and how well you have taken care of her."

"Don't worry about Liza. You just take care of things there."

They both said goodbye, and Scott felt more at ease knowing his daughter was in the hands of people who cared about her.

She did finish her finals and rushed home immediately after the last test. She grabbed her things she had packed the night before, said goodbye to the Wilsons, and rushed out the door. Again her trip home was a duplicate of the one taken upon Henrietta's demise, without the crying. She was saddened, but she had already done the crying, and now she was concentrating on and planning for the funeral.

When she pulled into the driveway and entered the house, she immediately wanted details. "How and when did it happen?" she asked.

Her mother took it upon herself to furnish the details. "Grandpa found her Monday morning. Annie was bleating so loud and continuously, and he knew something was wrong. He went out to the porch and saw Nanny lying still as Annie stood over her, bleating. He called us because he was not that steady even with his walking stick and felt uncomfortable walking into the corral by himself. Your father had just left for work, so I rushed down there. But when I found I couldn't move Nanny and Grandpa couldn't help, I called your father at work. He was able to get someone to cover for him and, in a couple hours, joined us. We put her in the storage shed. Liza, Annie stayed with her and followed us clear to the gate. She never stopped bleating. She knew something wrong and wanted help. She stayed to protect her, a true friend to the end."

"But how were you able to preserve her? I know you couldn't just leave her in the shed."

"Andy was able to help us convince the morgue at the hospital to let us keep her there. We were lucky there were no tenants at the time. He had to pull a few strings, but fortunately, he finally talked them into it. But we have to have her out of there by tomorrow morning."

"Then we should get Grandpa's truck and pick her up now."

"It is late," her father said. "I don't think they would let us in at this hour. Besides, what could we do tonight? It will be better if we keep her there until morning, when we can take care of her. Tonight you need to get some sleep, and we'll make arrangements in the morning. Grandpa and I have already made a casket and marker for her. We have also dug a grave next to Henrietta. Andy has expressed a desire to attend the ceremony, if that is all right with you. Now your mother has prepared something for you to eat, and you need to get to bed."

"But, Dad, I need to see her."

"It is too late. Now I am still you father, and I expect you obey me as long as you are in my house. Now, please, honey, do as I tell you." Then he gave her a smile and a big hug. There was no more discussion, and they finally all went off to bed. Liza was so tired from staying up late the night before, cramming, up early for tests, and then the long drive. Despite everything going through her head, she fell asleep in short order.

The next morning, they were all up early, and, after a quick breakfast Liza wanted to skip, they were in the car, headed to the farm to pick up Roger's truck. There was already a tarp in the back. Andy pulled up in his car, and, as he got out, Liza ran to him and put her arms around and started weeping. "It's all right," he said. "Everything will be all right. We will get through this. It is, as Grandpa always says, the regular cycle of life that we have to endure. We'll get through it together." Then he turned to her father. "I thought you could use my help."

He was always around when needed. He knew handling Nanny would be a two-person job, and Roger couldn't help, although he would try. Liza would be too emotional, and Jean not really strong enough. Besides, since he was instrumental in checking Nanny in. He would naturally be the one to sign for her release. All thought, officially, she was never there.

Jean stayed with Grandpa, as Liza and her father and Andy piled into the pickup. Despite Liza's urging to hurry, her father drove cautiously. It was an old truck, and there was a law against speeding. When they arrived at the hospital, the morgue attendant was happy to see them and anxious to get rid of their guest. She was enclosed in a plastic zipper bag, which Scott and Andy left closed, and they carried Nanny to the pickup and placed her in the bed on the tarp. Liza wanted to unzip the bag, but her father convinced her to wait until they got home. When they got to the farm, Jean and Roger were waiting for them on the porch swing. They backed the truck up to as close as they could get to the burial site to avoid carrying Nanny any further than they had to.

They took Nanny's remains directly from the back of the pickup to the burial site. Everyone followed, and as soon as they got there, Liza said, "Give me a minute. I need to prepare, but I need to see her one more time before we bury her."

Then she knelt beside the covered body before she unzipped the covering. Then she slowly unzipped it, exposing only the head which she reached over for and held in her hands. "We have to say goodbye, old friend. You were my best friend, and I will miss you greatly, but I will never forget you." Then she turned and looked at her father and nodded her head. She was determined to be strong and struggled to hold back the tears.

Andy and Scott removed Nanny from her covering and placed her in the wooden casket her father and grandfather had previously made and then placed her in the previously dug grave. Roger insisted on placing the grave marker he had made himself. Jean stood by to steady him. It was a family funeral, and everyone played a part. After filling in the dirt, there was a time of silence as everyone prayed or gave their thoughts in silence. No formal sermon was offered. In a short while, the men started gathering the tools and plastic tarp and headed back to the house with Jean alongside. Liza remained, as she did with Henrietta, expressing her emotions in silence.

They all knew nothing they could say would improve the situation for Liza. "She's taking it hard," her mother said. "But she's trying to be strong. But no matter how hard we try, or how much psychology we implement, the emotions will come out. Their relationship was so deep she is going to take time to adjust. We need to give her space and, when she is ready, let her come to us."

"That goat meant a lot to me as well," Roger said. "After all, she was my friend and companion before she was Liza's. I can understand how she must be taking it. You couldn't help getting attached to her, and Liza's relationship went beyond just friendship."

Finally, Jean spoke up, "I'll get something to eat. I'm sure we all could have some breakfast."

"A good idea," her husband said. "I doubt anyone is really hungry, but we have to carry on with life and keep our strength up. Andy, please stay and join us. I'm sure your presence will help Liza feel more comfortable and at ease. After all, you two have become like brother and sister, and sometimes siblings can comfort and understand where parents can't."

Shortly, they were enjoying a breakfast of ham and eggs and toast. Soon after they sat down, Liza walked in. "Sit down and join us for breakfast," Roger told her.

"I'm not hungry."

"I didn't ask if you were hungry. I said sit down and eat something." Apparently, he did not hear or listen to Jean's earlier advice. As usual, he was handling things his way, facing them head-on. She happened to be standing next to him, and he stood up without help and gave her a big hug. "We all loved Nanny, and we will endure her departure together as a family. Now it is time to sit down and eat as a family, so sit down and eat."

Liza could only smile through her watery eyes. Grandpa was taking charge, as he usually does, in times of stress and pressure. And she realized that was one of the qualities she admired about him. He would always be there to take charge, like he did on the day they first met. She sat down and joined them without another word.

When everyone got their fill and everything was cleaned up, they all departed for their own homes, leaving Grandpa alone to go over his own feelings alone.

That evening, as Liza had retired to her room, Jean said, "How does he do it?"

"Do what?" Scott responded.

"With just a few words and a hug, Grandpa not only took charge but seemed to bring Liza out of her quandary."

"After all this time, you are surprised? How many times has he stepped in to control situations? Sometimes it has been subtle, and we didn't even notice. But other times, it feels as if he hits us over the head with a brick. But he does it and always will. And for one, I am thankful for it."

"I know you are right, but it still amazes me."

The next day, Liza returned to the farm to visit Nanny's final resting site. While standing there, Roger walked up behind her, supported by his walking stick. "You know, that is not a proper grave marker. I was a little rushed but felt we had to have something at the time. I think it would be proper is you designed and built her a proper marker. Come on down, let's get started." She knew his walking to the grave site was a struggle for him. Even with his walking stick, it would take great effort. She then walked with her arm around him for support as they walked down to the house.

When they reached the house, he said, "Let's go inside, and you can use my living room desk to draw out plans." As Liza worked on her project, her grandpa took a nap on his lounge chair. The walk had tired him out. She drew a few ideas before she came up with something she was satisfied with. She ended up with a simple- shaped gravestone marker but with Nanny's name engraved on it and a replica of a goat inlayed below it. Below that were the words "our best friend." No dates were included since she never knew Nanny's birth date, and, to her, Nanny would be with her forever. She turned to show Roger but noticed he was fast asleep and decided to let him nap a little longer. She decided to gather eggs and feed Annie in the meantime. By the time she got back, Grandpa was in the bathroom. When he came out, she showed him the plans. "Very good, princess. Now let's go into the shop, and we can begin making your idea a reality."

Liza smiled, not just because they were going to make a grave marker for Nanny but also because it had been a long time since he had addressed her as princess, the nickname he gave her when they first met. When they reached the new shop, the one created after the remodeling, he inquired of her, "Now you have to select the types of wood you want to use. Remember, any inlays are to be in a different color of wood so it stands out. He had instructed her on woodworking previously, so she was not totally lost. She also knew that, without his guidance, she would have no hope of accomplishing her project.

It took three good days to complete the marker. There was a lot more measuring, gluing, cutting, sanding, and finishing than she had figured there would. She realized how much work and time her Grandpa had put into all the items he had made for them and others. It gave her a new appreciation of woodworking, a hobby her father now was learning and enjoying. They had to put three coats of finish on it so it could withstand the weather better. Nothing would prevent weather from taking its toll, Roger explained, but it would delay it. She did most of the work while Grandpa sat in a chair, supervising and, at times, showing how things were done. When finished, they replaced the old marker with Liza's new one together. This time, there were smiles and not tears at the grave, and they gave each other a big hug. "It is beautiful," Liza remarked.

"You did a wonderful job, princess. I'm proud of you. And Nanny, I'm sure, is proud of you too."

"We, we did a wonderful job," she said.

As it was late when they placed the marker, Liza waited until the next morning to invite her parents and Andy to see it. It was a Saturday, so her father and Andy would not be working. It was to be a surprise. Her and Roger were the only ones who knew anything about it. It was to be a surprise for everyone else. When she invited the others to join her and Roger at the grave site, they had questions, but Liza just told them it was a surprise. When they arrived, the marker was covered by a gunnysack.

Roger spoke up as they were all talking, wondering why they were there and why the marker was covered. He reached down, took hold of the sack, and pulled it off. They were all in awe. "Liza wanted to place a proper maker for our friend. She made it herself."

"Grandpa, you know it was your idea, and, without your help and guidance, I couldn't have done it."

"I think it is wonderful," her mother exclaimed.

"I have been working with wood for a while with Grandpa's instruction, and I don't think I could have done as good a job," her father said.

Andy just stared at it with his mouth open. Finally, he commented, "I think you have found a new talent. I want you to make one for me when I go."

At that, everyone laughed, and, with more compliments and talking, Jean noticed Roger wavering. Even though he was propped against a tree, being on his feet for very long weakened his legs, and they would give out. "Here, we better get you back to the house so you can get off your feet." She then put his arm over her shoulder and her arm around his waist and walked him back to the porch, where she placed him in the swing. She sat next to him. "You know, I must be getting old too, I'm tired."

"Who are you calling old?" he replied.

"You, you old goat."

This was the same old exchange they went through on a regular basis. It was their way of saying "I love you," and they were family. The others were there and heard their banter. Andy didn't take it as funny, but Liza and her father burst out laughing. They had to explain verbal banter to him, but they could see he still didn't quite get it. Roger and Jean started tickling each other and continued calling each other an old goat and nanny and laughing. This family had relationships with each other, like the one Liza had with Nanny, that others couldn't understand. But it worked for them, and they knew now what happened they would support and be there for each other. They shared a love and respect for each other seldom found, and they were happy.

Chapter 30

The Celebration

One afternoon, Scott stopped by Rogers to check in on him and see if there was anything he could help with. Jean was working that day. She still filled in when they needed, more out of courtesy rather than a need for the additional income, but it did help. Scott was now working part-time, three days a week and on call. This happened to be one of his days off.

As he drove into the driveway, he noticed Grandpa was not on the porch swing, which was usually where you found him. So although it brought a little concern, he walked into the back door and yelled, "Grandpa, Grandpa! Where are you?"

"I'm in the shop, and you don't have to yell so loud. I'm old, not deaf."

As Scott walked into the small shop, Roger was cleaning up. Not just a general sweeping and dusting but a deep type of cleaning. There were no projects out that he was working on and no tools on the workbenches. Everything was neatly put away in their assigned drawers, cupboards, and shelves. In fact, there were few finished items on the shelves as there usually were.

After looking around in amazement, he said, "What is going on?"
"What do you mean, what is going on? Can't you see I am cleaning the place up?"

"But you are usually working on some project, which I usually help with. And you never clean it this thoroughly and don't put all the tools away. And where are the finished projects we usually store on the shelves?"

"I sent the toys out to be distributed. Andy came and got them for me. I figured it was time to begin with a nice, neat, and clean workspace for our new project."

"A new project? You never mentioned anything about a new project."

"Oh, I guess I forgot to mention it to you. By the way, when is Jean's birthday?"

"You know very well when her birthday is. We have told you before. What does that have to do with you cleaning the shop so thoroughly?"

"Oh, I guess I forgot that too."

Scott looked at him with a questioning look on his face.

"It is June 25. Now, will you tell me what is going on?"

"Let's see. Today is April 4 today. We have to get busy."

"Are you implying that we are going to make something for Jean's birthday? But why clear everything out and do thorough housekeeping?"

"We need all the room we can get and won't have any time for anything more than a rough cleanup. We are going to have to keep things neat as we go."

"Just a minute," Scott said as he took Roger by the shoulders, handled him to one of the work chairs, and sat him down. "Now, let's begin again. What is the project we will be working on for Jean's birthday?"

"Well, a dining room table, of course." Looking at Scott as if he should have known.

"But we have a perfectly good dining room table at home."

"Not for your house, this house."

Scott was still a little confused.

"You have a suitable table as well. But if you want to replace it with a homemade table, I'm game. But how is that a birthday present for Jean?"

"I don't want to replace anything. We are going to make a large one for the living room and make it a dining room. My kitchen is not large enough to accommodate my growing family."

Scott just looked at him with more questions than answers. He thought to himself, *Is this the same recluse that would not allow people on his property and refused to let anyone in his house?*

"But there are only four of us, and your table is big enough for us." "Four, do you remember when Andy joined us for dinner here, and we had to squeeze together? Andy has a mother. Her name is Beth. And as my grandson, that makes her a part of my family. Do you intend to have everyone squeeze around a table that isn't even large enough to hold the dishes and food? And what about Andy's fiancé? I believe her name is Arial?"

"Okay, okay, you made your point."

"I want everyone to be able to sit down and enjoy a meal as one big happy family."

"Okay, I get it. It's just this is not the Roger I have grown to know and love and call Grandpa. You have caught me off-balance."

"It's all your family's fault. You and all your talk of love and family, and that includes my grandson Andy."

"You are the one that taught us. You taught us the true meaning of love through honesty, respect, self-respect, and all that goes with it. It was you that taught us to work, play, and grow together. You taught us the jots and rewards of accepting and helping each other. You are the one who gives and keeps on giving."

"Enough talk. Are you going to stand there flapping your gums, or can we get to work making a table?"

Scott then put his arms around Roger in the chair and, with a little chuckle, said, "We all love you, Grandpa, even though you can be a grump at times."

Roger turned and looked up at him and said, "I love you too, son." He gave him a smile and said, "Now, let's get to work."

They started by making up plans. There was little to no descent. Roger knew what he wanted, and Scott was only there to support his ideas, which he approved anyway. They came up with a tabletop that would be four feet by six feet, large enough to accommodate ten people comfortably. It would have rounded corners with the edges beveled and routed with a decorative pattern. It would be one solid piece with no leaf. There would be no corner legs to get in the way. Instead, there would be one centered pedestal with four legs with feet carved into the shape of lion feet. The entire table would be made of 100 percent solid oak that had been harvested from the forest behind his property. Fortunately, they had accumulated enough logs a couple of years ago to complete the project. Looking back and seeing the supply of oak, Scott came to realize Roger had been looking forward to when he accumulated the wood. At the time, however, he thought nothing of it because oak was Rogers preferred wood to work with. Now it had to be cut into boards, milled, and rough-finished before cutting into usable lumber. Roger had the tools to do the work, but it would be at least a two-man job, and Roger was in no condition to safely help.

Roger could measure and mark out and even cut some of the boards once they had a rough finish, but at this point, another set of able-bodied hands was needed. Andy was the first and really the only prospect. When approached, he was more than willing to help out after his city duties were completed and on weekends. Although he knew of Rogers's woodworking required finished wood, he wondered about the large quantity they were processing. When he inquired, he was told it was for a large project for someone special in town and was to be a surprise, so they asked him to not mention to anyone what they were doing.

Jean was another complication. They could only work on the table when she was not around. They had to be careful to make sure she didn't even see the material. She was familiar enough with their woodworking projects that to know the quantity was way beyond the usual projects and would ask questions they preferred not to answer. Luckily, she was spending more time at the store since the regular workers were on maternity leave with complications. They still had to be careful to make sure she was not around when working on it. With Andy's help, they were able to turn all the rough trees into workable lumber. At that point, they thanked him and said they could handle things from there on.

Now the measuring and cutting began in earnest. Scott concentrated on the tabletop, while Roger concentrated on the pedestal and feet. They often had to work together when it came to gluing things together, or it took someone to hold something while the other worked on it or had to do some adjusting. Most of the work Roger worked on, he could do in his shop chair, working at a workbench, but at times, he had to be on his feet. He never complained, but Scott was constantly telling him to sit down and take it easy. Scott could tell by the work done that was done during his absence that he was not taking it easy when he was working alone, and he worried about him.

The work was hard, intensive, and dirty, but after each work session, they gave each other a hug and smiled, feeling on top of the work because they knew it was a labor of love that made them feel warm inside. They eventually had everything put together and with a rough finish. Now it came down to the finishing work of sanding and finishing a very time-consuming and boring job. They had been able to keep the project secret, fortunately, and it was placed on top of the pedestal, and they made sure everything had fit properly and was level. This they did in the shop, where the door was kept closed to avoid wandering eyes. The top was pretty heavy and too heavy and awkward for one person to handle, so even though he struggled, Roger was forced to help. At these times, Scott worried, but Roger insisted he was fine. Things were really taking shape, and they disassembled the table to complete the finished work, knowing they would have to move and reassemble it in the living room when the time came. Scott was concerned Roger would be up to it. Assembling it was one thing; Moving was another.

The next item they had to address was food preparation for the dinner without involving Jean or making her suspect a dinner was planned. Again, they called on Andy for assistance when they informed him of their plans for a surprise birthday party for Jean. Understanding the situation, he was more than happy to help. He considered Jean a second mother, and to be left out of the preparations would have been an insult. When Roger insisted his mother and fiancé were to be invited, Andy was quick to offer their help in preparing for the fool needed. He knew his mother had been looking forward to meeting Roger for years and was anxious to do something for him but never knew what or how to approach him. This was the chance he knew she would jump at. When Andy approached her, she was all excited, like Andy had never seen her before. In fact, Andy could not get another word in as she went on and on with plans she was working up in her head. When he told her Arial was also invited, she got even more excited. She knew Arial enjoyed cooking and entertaining, and that was one of the things Andy liked about her.

"I'm going to call Arial right now," she said and wasted no time getting to the phone.

When Arial answered, and Beth explained the situation and invitation, she was a little in shock because she had never met Roger and felt a little out of place. However, Andy convinced her that he was his grandpa and that he would consider her a part of the family as well, even though they were still unmarried. Between Beth and Andy, she was finally convinced she would not be an outsider and agreed to team up with Beth on the project.

"If you have questions, you can go through me. But you two will be in complete control of the menu and preparation. Another thing, Roger has very little serving dishes or silverware, so you may need to make arrangements there as well."

"It's okay, Andy. Leave it to us. We'll take care of everything. We only have four days to get things done. We have a lot to get done."

His mother shooed him out of the house.

Liza, of course, was informed of the party and planned to come down from school after classes on Friday, which was the actual day of her mother's birthday. The party was planned for the Saturday after so everyone, including Liza, could attend. So everyone was informed except the guest of honor.

Roger and Scott worked overtime but were able to finish the table two days early. Now everything was set with all involved and informed of the time and date. They were all having trouble biting their tongue to keep Jean from finding out or becoming suspicious. They were all on pins and needles with excitement, but Roger and Scott were still the only ones who knew about the table. Everyone was told to withhold gifts and that this was a celebration for the family and a birthday gift for Jean.

The Friday Liza was to arrive home, Scott told Jean he was going to the farm to check on Roger while she got things ready for Liza's arrival. That sounded logical to Jean and thought nothing of it. However, the real purpose of the trip was to move the table and set it up in the living room. He knew it would not be easy, but when he got there, Roger was rearing to go and all excited. He seemed to have energy Scott had not seen in weeks, and they were able to move and reattach everything. It was a little struggle, but they were well pleased with the results. They took a well-needed little rest, and then Scott prepared a small meal for himself as he covered the table with a tablecloth he had picked up in town.

Liza arrived that evening as they expected. Jean had an evening meal prepared, and after they finished, they had their usual conversation on Liza's visits home to catch up, and they prepared to go to bed, except for Jean, because she returned to the kitchen.

"What are you doing?" Scott said.

"You know very well what I am doing. The same thing we do every time someone has a birthday. I'm going to bake a cake for tomorrow."

"Not this year. You are going to come to bed, and you are going to sleep in like the rest of us. Liza has a long drive home and longer day. She needs some sleep, and it wouldn't hurt us ether."

"But…"

"No buts. Now get in here before I give you a spanking here and now."

Jean gave him a scowl but followed him into the bedroom.

"You are impossible."

The next morning, after a good night's sleep, Jean was informed they were going to celebrate her birthday at the farm with Roger since he was still uncomfortable eating any place else. She was surprised but not suspicious.

"I guess I better get over there and get things prepared. It's getting late. I figured we could eat at about two. I think we can get things all prepared by then. Come along, Liza, I will need your help."

"Mom," Liza broke in. "This is your birthday. You are not going to lift a finger. Besides, Grandpa has taken care of everything."

"Excuse me. I know he is capable of preparing his simple meals, but I do not want his 'simple meal' for a birthday party, mine, or anyone else's. We will just go down there and take care of things and make sure we have a proper birthday dinner."

"Mom, I said things are taken care of. Dad and Grandpa are taking care of everything. Now put your jacket back on and relax."

"Your father can't find his way around the kitchen any more than Grandpa. They are both inept when it comes to preparing a decent meal, and I certainly don't want you spending your time off school waiting on me."

"Excuse me," Scott broke in. "Who are you calling inept? No help in the kitchen. I take offense to that remark." Liza had to giggle at that. "We two inept individuals, for your information, have taken care of everything, and you and Liza do not have to do anything but enjoy the meal."

But Jean wouldn't let it go.

"What did you do order out?"

"I've got a lot in mind to call everything off with that attitude," Scott replied.

Liza had never experienced this attitude from her parents before and knew it was time to use her psychology training to good use.

"Mom, Dad, calm down. You two sit down on the couch and listen to me. I know both of you have been through a lot of stress lately, and my being away has not helped. Mom, believe me, you will like your birthday, and the food will be great. I know you trust me. So trust me now. Everything is under control, and Dad and Grandpa know what they are doing. Now I want you to give each other a big hug and kiss. And Mom, you need to say you are sorry. Dad has been working hard to make this the best birthday you have ever had. Have a little faith."

"You have been planning this? For how long?" Jean said as she turned to her husband. Then she turned to Liza, "And you knew about this and didn't tell me?"

"Mom, a surprise is not a surprise if you let the person being surprised to know about it."

"But we haven't had a surprise party before. Why now?"

Scott cut in. "We haven't had a grandpa like the one we have before either."

"So he is the one behind this?"

"He was the one to set things in motion, but it was a mutual endeavor. Now we are expecting about one, so do what you have to do and no more questions. And please act surprised."

"Honey, I am so sorry and ashamed. But you know, I was mostly kidding, and it got out of hand. I love you so much just for who you are and everything you do for me and Liza."

She gave him another big hug and a kiss.

When they arrived at Roger's, Jean noticed Andy's car in the driveway.

"Is Andy joining us?" Jean asked.

"No more questions, remember?" Scott said.

As they walked into the kitchen, she was met with a group of people who yelled, "Surprise!"

She fell back against her husband with her hands over her open mouth. When people started clapping and coming up to her to give her a hug and wish her a happy birthday, tears began to form. She now really regretted the hard time she gave her husband the night before. She was so ashamed of herself that it made her even more emotional, and the tears wouldn't stop.

Scott gave her a hug and said, "It's not that bad."

"Not that bad," she said through teary eyes. "It's wonderful. How did you do it, you wonderful man? I will never doubt or tease you again. Do you forgive me?"

"I can't take all the credit. As I said, the whole thing was Grandpa's idea. I just helped make it happen."

Then she noticed Roger calmly sitting at his kitchen table. She walked over and gave him a big hug and a big smile.

"You are the best grandpa ever. But I don't understand, this is not like you."

"I guess you still don't know what I am really like. But you're right about who I was. But you changed me. But don't get too comfortable with the new me."

"The old you, the new you, I don't care. I love you. You are the best."

"Enough of this mush. We have guests and a party to get started."

Jean turned around; she had almost forgotten about everyone else. She noticed all the food on the table.

"Where did all this food come from, and how are we all going eat around this tiny table?"

Andy spoke up, "We enlisted a couple of pairs of extra hands, you know."

"Arial and I were glad to pitch in, especially for the woman who, years ago, knocked on my door and changed me and Andy's lives forever. I almost threw you out, but you persisted, and I am so thankful you did. Happy birthday. We love you."

Jean gave them both a big hug and said thank you, but she couldn't stop the tears.

Scott interrupted things when he announced in a loud voice, "Since we all agree this table is inadequate, I suggest we all retire to the living room, ah, dining room, where it will be more comfortable."

As they did so, they all noticed a large covered object, obviously a table, with eight chairs around it. He then grabbed the tablecloth and gave it a yank.

"Happy birthday, honey, from Grandpa and I."

As the table was exposed, everyone gave oohs and aahs, along with remarks on how beautiful it was. It had been finished to a shiny finish that looked like glass. The grain of the wood stood out in a beautiful pattern. Again, Jean covered her mouth with her hands in shock.

"Grandpa, I don't believe it. But how did you manage it without me knowing about it?"

"I didn't do it alone. Your husband did most of the work. I mainly supervised. Andy also helped."

At that, Andy spoke up, "I'm innocent. I didn't know what I was doing."

At that, everyone laughed.

Scott again spoke up, "Don't let him kid you. It was Grandpa's idea and project from the beginning. He worked night and day on it. He would fall asleep with a sanding block in his hand, slumped on what he was working on. I had to put him to bed more than once."

"That's my grandpa," Liza said.

She then walked over to his recliner, where he landed, and gave him a big hug. Jean followed suit.

"And the chairs are so beautiful and match perfectly," Jean commented.

"We can't take credit for them," Roger said. "Scott was able to pick them up at a furniture store in town."

Scott added to Roger's remarks, "Although I'm sure Grandpa could have made the chairs, there was no way we could have accomplished in less than two years making each by hand."

"I still don't believe you were able to complete such a project without my knowledge. And how did you manage to move it by yourselves? It must weigh over a hundred pounds." Jean asked.

"We managed. You would be surprised by how strong and resourceful our grandpa is when he wants to be. I was worried about him myself, but he seemed to have an inner strength because of the love he put into it."

Finally, Roger spoke up, "Enough talk. I'm hungry. Let's get some food on the table so we can all sit down and eat. Andy, will you help me out of this infernal chair? Every time I sit down in it, it wants to swallow me up."

Everyone promptly went into action. The tablecloth was returned to cover the table, and everyone chipped in to get the dishes and food on the new table. Arial, coming from a larger family, had furnished a set of dishes large enough for the gathering. Beth and Arial thought of everything. They realized how much joy they had working together. It provided a time to get to know each better and build a strong friendship and bond.

When everyone was seated with Roger at one end of the table and Scott at the other end, Roger stood up, supported with his hands on the table.

"I want to welcome everyone here today to celebrate my favorite daughter's birthday."

Jean interrupted, "As far as I know, I am your only daughter." That brought a little giggle from the others.

"Hush," he said. "Or you may not be for long."

That brought out more snickers. With a scowl on Jean's face, he went on, "This table is the representation of unity and family love. It was built as a present for Jean, but it is also my way of welcoming my whole family to be united, and I consider all of you part of my family. We have two people here today that have never been here before, and I want them to know I welcome them to the family and that this home and property are open to you at all times. At this table, we will share a meal, but we are here to share the love. Welcome family. Now, even though you know I do not believe in any formal religion, I would like to ask a blessing over this food and family." At the end of the prayer, he continued, "Now, let's make this food disappear so I can take a nap."

Again, Liza, as well as the others, had to hold in a laugh.

Then the clinking of silverware and dishes was heard as it would at any other family dinner. There were conversations, laughter, and smiles, along with a few lingering tears. And over it all sat an old man at the head of the table with a big smile on his face as he put away the food.

Liza sat quietly, thinking to herself how much she missed her grandpa. She knew she would never take him for granted or be shocked by his surprises. He was surely unpredictable but in a wonderful way.

When everyone had their fill and started to clean up, Roger, with help from Liza, retired to his room for a nap as promised. As he closed the door to his room for the nap, Jean looked at the door with tears again in her eyes and thought to herself, *You deserve it. Sleep well. I love you so much, you old goat.*

Soon everything was cleaned up; Beth, Arial, Liza, and Jean washed all the dishes by hand since there was no dishwasher in the house. They dried them and packed them away in the boxes that Arial brought in. Andy loaded them in the car. After another hour or so of visiting with all getting to know Arial better, they decided that it was time to go home. Andy had planned to take Arial home and help with the dishes before he and his mother returned to their home.

On the way, Arial commented, "I thought you were exaggerating when you told me stories about Roger. I believe everything you said now. What an amazing individual. I bet there is never a dull moment with him around."

"That is an understatement. I only hope he is around for you to get to know him better. He is the most loving and sharing individual I have ever met. He would do anything for you."

Beth spoke up, "That is another understatement. Maybe someday you will find out the whole story, but today is not the day."

The Petersons lingered on to make sure everything was cleaned up and in order. Jean had to take the tablecloth off to take home to be washed. In doing so, she stood there for an extended period of time to admire the table.

When her husband walked up behind her, put his hands on her shoulders and his down next to hers, she commented, "I still can't believe you did this. It is so beautiful."

"No more beautiful than the woman I married."

Chapter 31

The Dream Realized

Liza returned to school for her senior year. As usual, she was devoted to her studies and now was preparing for a graduate program. Another two years to get her master's.

Scott and Jean continued to spend a majority of their time at the farm. Roger's health continued to decline. They didn't know his exact age, but according to the doctors, he was in his nineties. He seldom suffered from ailments, but getting around was getting harder and harder, and he refused a wheelchair. He stuck to his walking stick, but it was not enough to venture outside past the porch without assistance.

Andy stepped in to help out and visit. Roger continued to work in his shop but was unable to work with the large power tools and raw wood. That task was taken over by Scott, who continued to learn under Roger's tutelage. Working side by side, they not only enjoyed the work but each other's company.

Scott continued to work at his job and had become a supervisor, so he was not on the streets anymore. Jean, having quit work years ago, spent almost all her time at Roger's, milking Annie, gathering eggs, feeding, and, in general, taking care of the animals. They had gotten rid of the bees, since Roger was the only one with enough knowledge to properly maintain them. Collecting the honey was an intensive chore no one wanted to endeavor. They missed the honey but knew some things had to go with the developing situation. They continued to maintain a garden, and Jean, with Roger's help and guidance, by now was not needed. They continued to can and preserve. They did their best to maintain Roger's lifestyle. They knew it was important to him and now became their lifestyle.

Liza visited home when she could. She now was working at a paid position at the hospital where she previously volunteered. It was on weekends and a few hours during the weekdays when needed. That prevented her from coming home as much as she would have liked to. She graduated with a BS in the top 5 percent of her class. She did come home for a couple of weeks before beginning graduate school.

Graduate school was even more expensive than college, and scholarships were not available. Her job at the hospital helped, but it was Grandpa who, as usual, stepped in. This time there was no argument. His physical condition was faltering, but his mind was as sharp as ever. He was well aware of situations. The university received a check from Roger's bank, approved by Darrell for the full year's tuition. Liza and her parents knew nothing about it until Liza tried to pay the first semester tuition. She was informed the full year was already taken care of. She also found out her room and board with the Wilsons was taken care of for the whole year. When she informed her parents, they just looked at each other, not in shock or surprise but respect and love. They were all one family now, and Roger took his position as the patriarch seriously, and it was not their place to question him. Besides, past experience proved it would do no good anyway.

Toward the end of her senior year, Andy and Arial were married. It was a fairly simple ceremony, and of course, Liza was the bridesmaid. Scott stood in as Andy's best man. Andy's first choice was Roger, but his inability to stand any length of time made it would have made it too uncomfortable. Besides, Roger still had his issues with being in public. He did, however, attend, observing from a chair in the back of the church in a dark corner.

They had been going together for so long; it wasn't a surprise. Andy had just been too busy previously to concentrate on the marriage as they wished. Arial had already been accepted as a member of the family, and it was just a formality. After the wedding, they decided to move in with Beth since that was where Andy was already living, and there was room there.

Chapter 32

The Scare

One Friday morning, after Liza had just began her first year of graduate school, Jean showed up at the farm at the usual time. She found Roger sitting at the kitchen table only badly, partially dressed. "You're late," he said.

Jean knew she arrived at the usual time and realized something was not the same with him. Despite his age, he usually had a sharp mind. He did occasionally forget things, but not much more than most people. He always was able to take care of himself without help and could do what needed done on his own. This greeting was completely out of character for him. "I missed you," he continued. And then he started to cry.

Now she knew something was wrong. "Here, let me help you get dressed. And then I'll fix you something to eat." She had to go to his room to get a shirt and socks and shoes.

"You fuss over me too much. We have a lot to do. Forget breakfast. I have to go to the bathroom, are you going to help me do that?"

She helped him up, but with his walking stick, he was able to make it to the bathroom on his own. She took this time to call her husband. "Scott, something is wrong with Grandpa. He is not himself. I don't know what to do."

"I'll be there as soon as I can. Call Andy, I may need his help. He can sometimes get through to him when we can't. Sometimes, being as close as we are is a disadvantage. Just humor him until we get there, and don't argue with him."

By the time she was off the phone, Roger was on his way back into the kitchen. Jean had retrieved the shirt, shoes, and socks while she was on the phone. "Here, let me help you to the recliner, and I can help you finish dressing."

"I don't want to get dressed. I think I'll go to bed. It's getting late. Where's Liza? I haven't seen her today. Will she visit me tomorrow?" He then shuffled into his bedroom, where he collapsed onto his bed, still in his pants. Jean pulled the covers over him, and he was fast asleep in the time it took her to leave the room.

She sat down at the kitchen table with her head down in her arms. She began to cry. She soon gained control of her emotions and thought to herself. *What would Grandpa do? He would do what had to be done.*

She then got up, retrieved the milk bucket, and went out to milk Annie. When she got back and put the milk in the refrigerator, she checked on Roger and found him still fast asleep. She knew the eggs had to be gathered, but that could wait. She hoped Andy and her husband would be arriving soon. Although she was trying to remain calm as Roger would, she knew it would be a matter of time before she gave in to her emotions.

Within ten minutes, Scott burst through the back door. "Where is he? How is he doing?"

"He's been sleeping for the last half hour. When I came in, he was at the table, partially dressed. I offered to help him finish dressing him and fix breakfast. He acted out of it and told me to stop fussing over him. I have been helping him get dressed for months now, and he always thanked me. Now he feels like I am intruding. He said he had to go to the bathroom, so I helped him up, and he walked in on his own. But when he came out, he asked where Liza was and acted like it was bedtime and went to bed. I covered him up, but that is where he is now."

Just as she finished, Andy rushed in. "I'm sorry, I was in the middle of a project and had to get someone to take over. How is he?"

"He's asleep, but according to Jean, there is definitely something wrong. Should we wake him up and take him to the hospital?"

"I think we should let him sleep and decide when he wakes up what to do," Jean said.

"I suggest we call a doctor at the hospital," Andy suggested. "Excessive sleep could be an indication of a serious condition that requires immediate attention. Being a member of the city council has its advantages. I know the doctor on duty. I'll give him a call."

When he got off the phone, after describing Roger's behavior, as Jean relayed it to him, he said, "They suspect it could be a brain hemorrhage or a slight stroke. They suggest we bring him in as soon as possible for tests."

Jean was now in her element as the mother hen. "You two get him up, and I'll get him dressed. I already have his clothes out that I tried to put on him earlier."

Andy and Scott gently took hold of Roger and eased him to a sitting position at the edge of his bed. He was still pretty groggy, and Jean managed to finish dressing him before he was fully awake. "Is Liza here? She said she would visit today."

"That's why we are getting you dressed. We are going to take you to see her," Jean lied.

"That's nice," he responded.

Then the two men put his arms over their shoulders and led him out the door and into the car without any objection. Jean ran around, gathering more clothes and making sure everything was left in order. When they got to the hospital, Roger was alert enough to recognize it. "Is Liza sick? You didn't tell me she was in the hospital."

When they opened the car door for Roger, there was a wheelchair waiting for him. They had been notified and prepared. "Good idea, rush me to Liza's room. This will be much faster."

When they stopped at the front desk to check in, Roger became agitated. "Why are we stopping here? Don't you know what room Liza is in? I'm here to see my granddaughter," he told the nurses.

When they wheeled him into an exam room, he became agitated again. "Where is Liza? I want to see Liza." He was yelling and tried to get away as they proceeded to put him in the bed to be examined. He was thrashing around so violently the attending nurse called for assistance, and Jean, Scott, and Andy were asked to leave the small room to give space for the newly arrived attendants. They eventually had to sedate him before he hurt himself. He kept yelling, "I want to see my granddaughter! Where is Liza?"

Outside the room, his family could hear his cries, and Jean began to shed tears for the person she considered her grandfather. Scott just held her close. Soon he quieted down, and a nurse came out. "The doctor will be here soon. You can retire to the waiting room. We will let you know as soon as we find out what is going on."

"Can't you tell us anything?" Jean said.

"I'm afraid we won't know anything until tests are run and the doctor has a chance to go over them. Please." And she directed them to the waiting room.

"We should call Liza," Jean commented after they were settled in the waiting room.

"No," her husband said. "You know how she would react. Let's wait until we find out what's going on."

"I'm sorry, I have to go. Like I said, I was in the middle something I must get back to," Andy said. "Let me know as soon as you find out anything"

They both thanked him and said goodbye as they gave him a hug. "He has sure turned out to be a very nice boy. He is always there when we need him," Jean remarked. "Do you know he is running for mayor this election? He is getting quite popular in the community, especially with business owners. They say he is one of the few city council members who actually listened. Boy was my first impression of him wrong. I questioned Grandpa's way of handling the situation, but not now. He knew what he was doing."

Scott knew she was just talking to get her mind off Grandpa's condition. He knew all about Andy's run for mayor. In fact, he helped him develop a platform. And as far as his character, they had covered that subject before. He just leaned over and gave her a hug.

Jean soon got up, wringing her hands, staring into space, and walked around. "What is taking them so long?"

"It has only been about forty-five minutes," Scott replied as he looked at his watch. "Let me get you something to drink. I saw a vending machine in the hall on the way here. What can I get you?"

"Some kind of orange drink will be fine, or whatever. You know what I like."

He then headed for the vending machine, leaving his wife to continue pace the floor. When he got back, she was still staring at the ceiling and pacing. He went to the front desk. "Have you heard anything about Mr. Peterson?" They used their last name because, as of yet, they still didn't know Roger's real last name.

"Sir, the doctor will be in as soon as there is something to report."

Two hours later, the doctor came in, and they were both on their feet in an instant. "I have some good news. Your father has suffered a mild stroke that was brought on by a blood clot in the brain. As it turns out, it was caught soon enough that we can avoid operating. I believe, with proper medication, we will be able to dissolve the clot. We would like to keep him at the least a couple of days to see how he responds to the medication. He has been sedated, but you can see him for a few minutes. Even when the sedative wears off, the medication will keep him under for a few hours. You might as well go home. If there is any change, we will let you know. You may visit him this evening. By then he will be awake and more coherent."

Jean, again in tears but smiling, joined her husband in thanking the doctor. They immediately called Andy but decided to wait to call Liza until later in the afternoon when she was out of classes. They would have more time to talk then and wanted to be informed of the situation before they visited him that evening. They wanted her to be aware of things and calmed down before they called from the hospital and let her talk to Grandpa. They knew that call, as long as Liza was calmed down, would be the best medication for him.

When they went home, it was to the farm. There was nothing to do at their house, since Jean kept it clean and in order, but there was always something to do at Roger's. There were animals to feed, eggs to gather, and the house to clean and straighten up. Because of his immobility, Roger was unable to maintain the place properly, and, to be honest, sometimes tended to be a little untidy. Jean was always picking up after him like a mother. She decided to first gather some personal items for their trip later for the visit. She had already taken a change of clothes when they took him in. The hospital would furnish all items he needed, but Jean, being Jean, wanted to make sure she took care of everything. Scott went out to feed the animals and gather eggs. When he came back in, Jean was rushing around, straightening up and moving things around, and talking to herself. "Settle down, he'll be fine. Let's get something to eat. Then there is gardening we can do to keep us busy. After lunch we can call Liza, and I want you calmed down when we talk to her."

"You don't know that. A blood clot in the brain can be serious." "You heard what the doctor said. Besides, running around in circles, worrying, will not change things. There are things to do, and keeping busy will keep our minds off the situation. Now let's have breakfast, or in this case an early lunch, and carry on as Grandpa would advise us to do."

She then stopped fussing around and joined her husband in the kitchen where they warmed up a stew Jean had made the day before. They worked in the garden, and Scott mowed the lawn as Jean went home to get the mail and grab a change of clothes to change into when they returned to the hospital.

They were aware of Liza's schedule and knew her classes for the day ended at three. By the time Scott finished the lawn and Jean returned, it was three. That gave them a little time to get cleaned up and go over how they would break the news to her.

They were both on the phone when they called her. "Hello," she answered. "I wasn't expecting a call from you today. But I'm glad you did. I have some good news. We had a special guest teacher in one of my stuttering classes today. He is considered one of the best in the field. After the lecture, I got to meet him. He invited me to an office, and we ended up having a very productive conversation. He invited me to go on lectures with him and work with me on a personal level. Isn't that exciting?"

"That is exciting," her mother responded with subdued excitement. Scott could tell his wife's emotions would be picked up on by Liza, so he took over the conversation. "We are very thrilled for you. It sounds as though you are gaining training and experience beyond expectations. We are so proud of you."

"Dad, Mom sounds a little subdued. Is there something wrong? Did something happen to Grandpa?"

"Yes, but it is not serious. He is in the hospital, and he is being treated."

"He's in the hospital? What happened? Why didn't you call me?" she was yelling into the phone, obviously upset.

"Calm down, Liza," her father said. "As I said, he is resting in the hospital. He had a small blood clot in the brain, but the doctors are treating it with medication. They said he should be fine in a week or with continued medication and rest. They said, since we caught it early, it is not likely to be serious."

"Not serious? Dad, you are forgetting my field of study. The brain, and its function, is a major portion of what I am learning. As far as the brain goes, nothing is 'not serious.' I will be home tomorrow."

Both of her parents shouted into the phone. "You will not!" Her father again took over, "Is that what you think Grandpa would want you to do? You have your studies and must keep it up. This is a crucial point for you. You have obligations there. We can take care of things here, and Andy and Arial are always around to help out. We are going to the hospital for a visit in about an hour. We'll call you from there so you can talk to him yourself. Please don't get him upset by insisting you come home. You know how he feels about your education. It has been a major priority for him. You need to remain calm. Tell him about your visit with that doctor and lecturing potential with him you mentioned. He would love that. He needs something right now to lift his spirits. We'll call you from the hospital in a few hours. We love you."

"I love both of you too. Talk to you later." And they all hung up.

When they arrived at the hospital, the reception desk told them they could go ahead to Roger's room. He was awake, and a nurse was with him. The nurse in his room told them they could visit, and the doctor would be in shortly. She then left, leaving them alone. They both gave him a hug. "You look a lot better," Jean exclaimed. "You gave us a scare. Don't do that again. Liza threatened to leave school and rush home."

"I hope you talked her out of it. And, for your information, I don't remember what I did or what happened. The doctor just told me I had to take some medication for my brain. He said he would wait until you got here to explain it, when we were all together."

"The nurse said she will be in shortly. They told us the general idea, but I'm sure the doctor has more information."

About that time, the doctor did arrive. "Hello, I'm Dr. Williams. I'm glad you're all here. First let me go over with you what we are facing. I assume you are family."

"Yes," Scott said. "He is our grandfather."

"There seemed to be a little confusion with his legal name upon check-in. I'm sure you have cleared that up. Our patient has insisted we just address him by his first name, Roger. So that is what I shall do. Anyway, Roger developed a blood clot to the head which put pressure on the brain. That pressure led to a minor seizure, and that, in turn, led to memory distortions and sleepiness. Fortunately, because of your quick response and care, it was caught early, and there was no nerve damage that led to any paralysis, a common result of strokes. We caught the clot before it grew and caused more damage. We are treating it with a drug that should shrink it. So far, it seems to be working. As you can tell, he is more coherent and wide awake."

"I am coherent enough to tell you I want out of this place. Now where are my clothes?"

Even though he still had an IV in his arm, he tried to get up, but Jean and Scott held him down. "I'm sorry," the doctor said. "I didn't say you were out of the woods yet. You are still under medication, administered through an IV. If you continue to show improvement and a scan shows the clot is shrinking, we can put you on the medication in pill form, and you can go home."

"How long will it be before we know?" Jean asked. She and her husband were still holding Roger down as he continued to struggle.

"I want out now. I feel fine."

"You may feel fine now. But these things take time, and clots as this can return if left untreated. We need to keep you a couple of more days, at least, before we can discharge you, and only then, if the scan shows substantial shrinkage. But you must remain calm. This agitation is not good for recovery, nor does it help relationships with hospital staff or peace of mind for your family. Now if you cannot calm down, I will have to order a sedative. I would not like that, and neither would you."

He then settled down, and Scott and Jean were able to release their hold on him. "Now that is better," Dr. Williams commented. "He still needs his sleep, so please cut your visit to less than two hours. I will be back later this evening and again in the morning. I assure you he is in good hands, and I am sure he will make a full recovery. If there are no more questions, I will leave you alone."

Roger and Jean both thanked the doctor as he walked out of the room. They then turned to Roger, who was still wearing a frown on his face. "You heard what the doctor said," Jean said. "You have to remain calm and get some sleep. The sooner you do, the sooner you can come home. Besides, we promised Liza we would call her when we got here so you could talk to her yourself. That was the only way we could keep her from rushing down here. Now you must speak to her in a calm voice, and don't let on there is any problem or you can't talk to her. I'm sure you don't want her leaving school."

"Are you blackmailing me?"

"If that is what it takes, yes. Now do you want us to make that call or not?"

"You drive a hard bargain. Go ahead and make the call. I'll be nice." And he gave them a sour look and stuck out his tongue.

Scott just laughed, but Jean said, "Very mature." At the same time, she turned to her husband. "Don't encourage him. You're just as bad as he is." That brought on more laughter from both men, and even Jean had to smile.

Jean then made the call, and when Liza answered, she said, "I have someone who wants to speak with you." And she handed the phone to their grandfather.

"Hello, princess. It's good to hear your voice. I want you to tell me everything that's going on."

"Grandpa, for one thing, I haven't said anything yet, so you hadn't heard my voice. Second, we are having this conversation so you can tell me what is going on with you."

"I am fine. Everyone is making a big deal out of my being a little tired."

"You are in the hospital! It is a big deal. You forget, Grandpa, my studies include a lot of medical training in the workings of the brain. Mom and Dad have told me enough to know your condition can be serious. You have to listen to the doctors and do what they tell you. When I come home, I want to see you at home giving us all a hard time. I don't know what we would do without you. Now promise me you will behave and do what you are told."

He could never ague with Liza. To him, the sun rose and set by her. "You are as bad as your parents. I promise, but I won't promise to like it. Now what is going on with you?"

"You are impossible." She then filled him in on her working at the hospital and being asked to go on speaking engagements with a doctor who had been a guest lecturer in one of her classes. He listened intently, taking it all in like a sponge. He was smiling and in a very good mood when a nurse peeked her head in the door and informed that visiting hours were over. When they checked the time, Liza had been on the phone with her grandpa for over two hours.

Jean took the phone gently from his hand and said, "We have to hang up now, Grandpa. It's time we go, and you need to get some sleep."

"But we are not finished."

She then told Liza they had to hang up because visiting hours were up. She and Scott both told her goodbye and put the phone to Roger's mouth and told him to say goodbye. When he put a scowl on his face and started to say something, Jean waved a finger at him and mouthed the words *you promised.* And he just said goodbye in a pleasant, happy voice. She hung up the phone, and they both again gave him a hug and said goodbye, promising to visit him again the next day. He did not look very happy but said goodbye in a sarcastic voice as they walked out the door.

The next day, Andy and Arial were with them. They had filled them in. So he knew what to expect when they got there. Fortunately, their doctor was at the front desk as they walked in, and he invited them into his office for an update. "I have some good news. Your grandfather, even as stubborn as he is, is responding quite well to the medication. If the scans show what I hope and the improvement continues, we should be able to release him tomorrow, which will be a relief for the staff. He has been a handful, I'm sorry to say."

"That is good news," Jean answered. We know he can be difficult at times, but it's because he is used to taking care of himself and not relying on anyone for help. He is very independent. Believe me, we know how stubborn he can be. But he is our grandpa, and he has a heart of gold and would do anything for anyone needing it."

Andy then cut in, "I can vouch for that."

"Well," the doctor continued, "as I said, I'm sure you can take him home tomorrow, but you must continue to give him the medication. I will write you a prescription. Make sure he doesn't miss taking them as prescribed. Now I'm sure you would like to visit him, but watch for flying bedpans or nurses running for their lives as you enter. We have tried to keep him sedated but knew you would be here, so he has been awake for a couple of hours now. Good luck."

They all thanked the doctor as they hurriedly left his office. They knew Roger could be a problem, but he had never acted out as the doctor prescribed. When they got to the room, Jean slowly opened the door a crack and asked, "May we come in?"

"I told you—oh, it is you. Sorry, I thought it was those vampires in white again. Did you come to take me home?"

"Look who's here."

At that, Andy and Arial asked, "Do we have to protect ourselves from flying objects?"

"Get over here, Mayor, and give me a big hug."

"I'm not mayor yet, but I would like that hug."

They then all quickly covered the distance to his bedside and gave him a big hug. "We hear you have been giving the staff a bad time," Jean said. You promised to be good."

"But they won't let me do anything, and they keep taking my blood and won't let me sleep."

"You are in a hospital. You aren't supposed to do anything. You are here to rest and get better, and the nurses are here to help you get better."

"I don't need their help. I am fine and would feel a lot better at home where you can take care of me."

He was almost in tears, and it brought water to her eyes as she gave him another hug. "I know. I miss you too. But the doctor says if you behave you can come home tomorrow."

"We all miss you, Grandpa," Scott added. "We need you. Please be nice to the staff. They are only trying to help you get better so you can come home."

"How can I get better when they are trying to kill me with their food?"

"It can't be that bad."

"Well, it's not, but it is not yours. I want to come home."

"The doctor said you can come home tomorrow if today's tests come out as expected," explained Scott. "But you have to be good and settle down or you'll have a heart attack, and we won't be able to take you home."

"And I need someone with his composure to help me in my run for mayor," Andy cut in.

"Now promise you will behave or we'll leave you here," Jean threatened.

"You won't dare." Then they all laughed, and he promised to be good.

They then had a good visit and kept him up on things going on at home and the things they were doing to keep the place up. Andy filled him in on his campaign and ideas to improve things in the community.

A lot of them, he and Roger had previously discussed. Andy, as the community was finding out, was open to ideas and suggestions from others no matter where they came from. Roger, Scott, and Arial had become his close advisors.

They did not call Liza, despite Roger's continued requests. She was in classes now, and there was nothing urgent she needed to know. They would call her later that evening from home about his scheduled release.

The next day, he was released, and things got back to normal. They made sure he continued to take the medication, which the doctor said they would continue for six months. At that time, they would evaluate his condition to see if they would have to continue or not. They also made sure he got more rest, as per the doctor's orders. As was his nature, he wanted to be involved in everything, even if it was only to supervise or watch. To help alleviate things, Jean and Scott would not only inform him on things going on but asked for his advice and pretended they needed his supervision. It helped him feel like he was still involved in the day-to-day activities. He spent a lot of time on the porch swing, but they had to watch him because he had a tendency to want to get up and help in the activities. He was not an invalid, but they made sure if he walked any distance, someone had to be at his side.

Chapter 33

A Plan for the Future

After being home for about a week, he called Jean and Scott over to where he was relaxing on the swing. It was on a Saturday, so they were both their taking care of the animals and property as well as watching over him. "I think it's time we made some final arrangements."

"Grandpa, I don't want to discuss it. You are not going to leave us, at least not in the near future."

"I'm not talking about my demise. I'm talking about the future for you and Liza and this property. I had a lot of time to think when I was kept hostage. Darrell, Andy, and I were able to make some legal and financial arrangements."

Scott, along with his wife, sat down beside him. "If you are making decisions for our future, don't you think we should be involved? We have always made decisions as a family before."

"I don't intend to leave you out of the decision-making. But there are certain things concerning legal matters that have to be taken care of so we can go forward with family plans."

"What kind of legal matters?" Jean cut in.

"For one thing, Liza will be graduating with a master's in speech therapy, and she will have to have a suitable clinic to conduct her business."

"But she hasn't graduated yet and will probably have to work at another office to start with."

"My granddaughter is not going to work for someone else. She is going to have her own establishment, and you will be her staff. In fact, the clinic will be a sanctuary for children, run as a family business. Now don't interrupt me."

Jean and Scott looked at each with questions on their faces but remained quiet as requested.

Roger continued, "As you know, this property has the status as a historical landmark, giving it tax advantages. As long as we keep its appearance as it is, it will remain so. Andy has vowed to set up the sanctuary as a tax-exempt charity, funded by private donations and with funding from the city. Darrell has drawn up papers to contribute this property to the charitable organization."

"But," Jean cut in, "I don't think Andy, as a council member, has that authority, and where will you live?"

"The election for mayor is in less than a month. At that time, Andy will become mayor. As a member of the city council, he has had enough influence to bring up the idea. And so far, the idea has been favorably accepted. As far as where I will live, it is up to you. You three will be the overseers of the facility, and you will own the property and business. Scott will be the caretaker for the grounds and animals. Jean, you will take care of the house and become an assistant to Liza, taking care of appointments, et cetera. And Liza will deal with patients and visitors in professional matters. This is to be a free clinic open to all who feel a need for friendly counseling or just need a place to get away. Contributions will be accepted, but the main funding will come from a private fund and one to be established by the city."

"Aren't you getting a little ahead of things?" Scott said. "Andy is not mayor, and Liza still has over a year of school to go. And, as Jean brought up, where do you fit in? Have you discussed any of this with Liza?"

"She has enough to worry about, and I know my granddaughter. I know of her desire to help others, and so do you. I don't want her to worry about the little things. I want her to be able to just step in and get to work doing what she was meant to do. She can use the living room and the desk in there as her office." I picture this as a place where no one is turned away and all are treated with love and friendliness. Some may only need is a place to relax and get away from things and enjoy life as a child. It will be a place designed for children facing issues of all kinds. I know there will be a lot of logistics to work out, but I know you well enough to know you will be able to handle them as they come up."

"It sounds as if you have worked things out," Jean said. "But I think it's a little ambitious. Have you discussed any of this with Liza? You still haven't answered our question of what about you."

"Liza will be the key. And I am sure she will want to make arrangements to suit her needs. I'm sure she has learned organizational skills with her training. Since you will all be CEOs of the foundation, you will be given a salary out of the funds provided. As far as me, I still will have my little room and bed and intend to help where needed, as long as you don't kick me out. My name will no longer be on the title of the property, and you three will have complete control of the facility. However, I suggest losing the bees. They probably would create an issue, especially with children."

"But this is your place," Jean insisted.

"Once everything goes through, it will belong to the foundation, which you will be in charge of. It would end up in your hands eventually anyway. And if at some time in the future you decide to dissolve the foundation, which would be your right, the property would revert to you. Now I am feeling a little tired. I think I will take a nap."

He then got up, with a little help, and, with his walking stick, proceeded to his bedroom. They watched him from the door to make sure he made it to the bedroom safely. He managed to get around without help fairly well within the house. Once he was in his room, they returned to the swing to discuss what they had just been informed.

They weren't sure what it all meant but knew one thing. They had to inform Liza of this new revelation, despite Roger's concern it could affect her studies. They felt she was already under the pressure of deciding what she would do after graduation. This information would be a two-edged sword. Now she would no longer have to worry about future plans after school. But this would present a new issue and a different pressure. They were also worried about their grandfather relinquishing all his assets for a dream. They were smart enough to figure out where the private fund was to come from. That would leave him with nothing. But as he made it very clear to them many times before, it was his money, and no one had a right to tell him what to do with it. Everything sounded so final, and that worried them. It sounded as if he no longer planned to be around. He was always the one in charge, and now he was scaring them.

Finally, Scott told Jean to stay with Grandpa. He was going home to give Liza a call. He didn't want Roger to overhear. When Liza answered and after the greetings and her father described what Roger had told them, she yelled into the phone, "But he can't do that!"

"I'm afraid he has set everything in motion, and Andy is helping him. We can't do anything about it. You know as well as I do we can't tell him what he can and can't do, especially when it comes to finances. He is convinced it is something you want and need."

"It is, Papa, but not like this. He will end up with nothing. That place has been his life. Without it he will—"

"Yes, honey. That is the same conclusion your mom and I came to. But you are only partially right. You are his life, and nothing is more important in his mind. His plan is his ultimate gift to you."

Scott could hear is daughter sobbing over the phone. "Liza, I know how you feel. But if we fought him on this, it would kill him. I know he means it as a surprise for you, so you can't say a word to him about it. Liza, we all love you. This is what he always wanted you to do. Complete your education, come home, and take charge of the clinic, or sanctuary as he prefers to call it. Believe me, we are just as concerned about the situation as you are. He always said you were special, now show it. Become the best therapist this town has ever seen."

He then said, "We love you, honey," and hung up the phone.

Liza was too emotional to say anything and continued to sob as she slowly hung up the phone.

Chapter 34

Final Act of Love

Andy was elected mayor as Roger predicted. He pushed through the paperwork that the council had been working on. It was a busy time for Andy. He had not only become mayor but his wife was expecting their first child. Their marriage had taken place two years earlier with Liza and her family in attendance. Andy's wife, Arial, had not yet met Roger but had heard a lot about him. Andy wanted to introduce them, and his work with him at this time provided a perfect opportunity. He felt the pressure to complete the applications and other paperwork to fulfill Roger's desires. A lot was done over the phone, but papers had to be signed and notarized, which required personal visits to the farm. Fortunately, Andy was also a notary, but some items required a witness, and that is where his wife came in.

Roger and Arial had hit it off since Jean's birthday party, but she was not aware of the circumstances which led to her husband and Roger's relationship. On the way home, after one of those visits, she asked him, "Why do you call him Grandpa? I know he is not your real grandfather."

"That is a long story. But as you learned at the birthday party, this is an adopted family of which you are now a part of. I'll give you the whole story someday, but now is not the time."

Andy was not the only visitor Roger had at this time. Darrell again accomplished a lot on the phone but had to obtain signatures, and, at times, a notary was again required. Again, Andy stepped in. Liza's signature would eventually be required on most of the documents, but that would have to wait. They all knew she would be reluctant at this time so decided to wait until she was ready or when it became necessary. Soon all preparations were completed for the transfer of property and assets and the establishment of a charitable foundation. The city council approved city funds to support the sanctuary, seeing the advantage it would be to the community.

But Roger had other projects as well. He was spending more than usual time in his shop, now referred to by the family as Santa's Workshop. Scott, who often worked with him in the shop, noticed him working on something new and different. But when he walked in, Roger would put it away. He realized it was something Grandpa wished to keep to himself.

Jean, knowing he was working on documents and provisions to facilitate the transfer of property and setting up the sanctuary, one day inquired, "When are you doing all this legal work? I am with you almost all day long, and you never are on the phone or have anyone over to sign papers."

"That is my business and is nothing you have to be concerned with. You will be notified when I'll require your assistance." He felt if they got involved in the legal matters, it would complicate matters. He knew what he wanted and had the proper legal advice necessary to get it done. So he pretended to be tired when it was still early and would tell her he needed to go to bed early. Then when she and Scott left for home, he would get up and call Andy or Darrell to go over things or have them come over as required. That led to him being tired during the day, and Jean just assumed it was because of his health or age. He, at times, would work in the shop on his special projects at night as well. He still liked woodworking, and that is one thing he could still do as long as it only required sitting at the workbench in the workshop. He had plans for something special and knew his time was limited.

Liza, fortunately, was busy with her studies and activities. She was now making regular appearances with the doctor. Although she had cut back on work at the hospital, she still worked there on weekends. Now with the information of her grandfather's plans, she was torn in so many directions she had to get counseling of her own. On one of those appearances, she mentioned her situation to the psychologist, and he sat down with her. They had a good talk. He had always been impressed with her. He gave encouragement and counseling that helped relieve the pressure. He said he would be there for her professionally as well as personally. It managed to relieve some of the pressure she was under. It made her more relaxed, knowing she had someone who cared and could talk to. It helped that he could help not only as a friend but be able to provide professional help as well. She felt she may need his advice in her future career as well as personally. It felt good to know he would be there.

At this time, Liza was attending school without a break now, trying to complete her degrees as soon as possible. She was determined to receive two master's degrees—one in speech-language pathology and one in child psychology. Graduate school allowed you to work at your own pace, and Liza was pushing herself. However, hearing of Roger's plans and his emotional state and health, she knew she needed to take time to go home.

She didn't bother informing her parents of her plans to come home. She just said goodbye to the Wilsons, saying she would be gone for about a week, and took off. Since she left early, she arrived at Alderwood late in the afternoon. She didn't bother going home. She went straight to the farm, where she knew her parents would be. When she pulled into the backyard, her father and grandfather were relaxing in the swing on the back porch. She flung the car door open, not bothering to close it, and ran with her arms open to the porch.

Her father was out of the swing in an instant, and they gave each other a big hug. "You didn't let us know you were coming. We missed you so much."

She then reached down to give Roger a big hug. He could not get up by himself, but he tried, and it did not prevent him from pulling her down to his level. "I love you, my little princess, and missed you so much."

In the meantime, Scott ran to the back door. "Honey, come out here. Look who's come home?"

Jean had been inside preparing dinner but, hearing the commotion, didn't wait for her husband's invitation. She came flying out the door, screaming, "Liza, is it really you?" She wasted no time joining them on the swing with hugs and kisses. "Why didn't you let us know you were coming?"

"I just decided on the spur of the moment. I woke up this morning realizing I could skip the scheduled classes I had without a problem. The weekend is coming up, and I needed to be home." It was a Friday which would give her at least three days and more if she wanted to stay longer.

Her father joined them all in the swing even though it was crowded. But no one seemed to mind. In fact, it seemed to be just perfect since everyone was in such a tight hug no one noticed. They were all smiles, and once the hugs were over, everyone started to talk at once. Liza held up her hands. "Hold on, I didn't come home to talk about what I am doing in school. I want to know what is going on here." At that, everyone shut up. They were afraid to bring up the topic. Finally, she continued, "I understand someone has been making plans for the disposition of this property and the establishment of a clinic that I am supposed to be in charge of."

"A sanctuary," her grandfather broke in. "It is to be a sanctuary for children. You will have a clinic in the sanctuary, but your parents will oversee the day-to-day operations and maintenance of the place. It will be a nonprofit organization free to visitors. It will be funded by city as well as private contributions. You will each receive a salary and jointly become managers as well as owners of the institution. I am not qualified to advise you on all the legal issues. You will have to discuss them with Darrell and Andy. They are more qualified to fill you in. Now that we have covered that, I want to know what is going on with you and your education."

Jean and Scott were in awe. They had not brought up the subject with Roger because of health reasons. Now he was laying it out without reservation or emotion. "Hold on a minute, Grandpa," Liza yelled as she jumped up out of the swing. "It sounds as if you have made a lot of decisions concerning my future, and assumptions that you have no right to make without my knowledge or input."

"You are right, but it is my right to do with my property as I wish. And it was to become yours one way or another. The foundation I propose to set up will be in your names, and you will have the right to do with it as you please or even abolish it as you wish. As far as a clinic run by you, I thought that was what you were going to school for. Remember, this sanctuary will be for children—all children, not only those with emotional issues but any who feel a need to be accepted and loved. Is there anything you object to that?"

Liza just stood there with her mouth open. She didn't know how to reply or object. He had apparently thought about everything. She couldn't think of anything in his plan she could really object to. What really made her mad was that he did it on his own, and apparently, he was leaving himself out of the future. That scared her.

As she didn't seem to object, he went on, "Before you return to college, there are some papers you will need to sign. Darrell and Andy have documents needing your signature to get things started. You can ask them any questions you may have at that time. I'm sure they will be able to answer any of your questions satisfactorily. Now I want no more business talk. I want to enjoy my family, and I don't need any talk to do that. Welcome home, honey." Then he reached out, grabbed her hand, and pulled her back down into the swing.

Jean suddenly jumped up and ran into the house. "I forgot I had something on the stove."

The others laughed, and Scott said, "I guess we all might as well go inside. If it's not burned, it's time for supper anyway." So they both helped their grandfather up and went into the house. Luckily, nothing was burned, and they all sat down to a family dinner they hadn't enjoyed for months.

After supper and everything was cleaned up, her parents went home, while Liza and Roger again retired to the porch swing. It was getting a little chilly, so Jean brought them a blanket before she left. They sat in the swing, snuggled together in the blanket. "I will give Andy a call in the morning," Liza remarked. "But tonight I just want to spend time with my favorite grandpa." At that, he gave her a little punch in the shoulder, and they both laughed. They talked of school and her activities there. They joked around, like they always did, reminiscing on the past and laughing. Yesterday was a long day, and it had been a long drive for Liza. It wasn't long before they both were asleep in each other's arms with smiles on their faces. When the cold woke Liza, it was after dark. She looked at her grandfather with tears in her eyes, not wanting to wake him. He looked so peaceful. But she finally did and helped him into the house and put him to bed. She knew that every time she visited, it could be the last to see him, and this time more than ever.

She did call Andy the next morning. It was social as well as business related. It gave her a chance to visit with Arial as well. She had never seen her in the mother-to-be state before, so her awkward remark on Arial's size brought laughter from them all. "Andy, you are going to be a father. Does that mean I'm going to be an aunt?"

"Since Arial doesn't have a sister, you will be her only aunt," Andy replied. After the social visiting, they got down to business, and he went over the documents, establishing the farm as a sanctuary, and all the ramifications involved in establishing the trust necessary for the foundation. He came up with terms and technical issues she never dreamed of. Grandpa was right. There were technical terms and issues that Andy had to explain that Roger did not understand. Andy was not a lawyer, but he had them at his disposal at city hall. He depended on them to draw up the documents, making sure everything was legal. After they went over everything and she signed where needed, he notarized things. He then called Darrell. Fortunately, he was available and offered to come to Andy's immediately. While he was on the way, they continued to visit. Liza filled them in on her studies. Andy and Arial related their experience of married life.

Darrell brought all the paperwork necessary to accomplish the transfer of the property and other assets of Roger's into Liza's name and the foundation. When he got there and they all made their greetings,

Darrell brought out the paperwork with a new deed to Roger's property with Liza's name on it. She had already signed the papers to make it a part of the foundation that would be in her family's name with her as the executor. She became emotional. "But by me signing these papers, it leaves Grandpa with nothing. I can't do that."

"I thought he had already gone over everything with you, and you were prepared? This is what he wants. He has been my friend before he met you. Believe me, he knows what he is doing, and by signing these papers, you will be fulfilling his dream."

Andy could see her reluctance. "Liza, you and I, more than anyone else, know Grandpa's heart. As Darrell said, he knows what he is doing. You are his dream. He has already given to us everything so we could fulfill our dreams. Now it's time for us to help him fulfill his. As I said before, you are his dream, but this sanctuary is also his dream. He wants you, your parents, me, and Darrell to fulfill and continue his passion."

"I know you're right, but it is so hard. What will he have? What will happen to him?"

"He will have us. The rest will be up to you. Now let's fulfill his dream before you have to return to school so you can fulfill another part of his dream."

She finally signed all the necessary documents, and Darrell gave her a hug, said his goodbyes, and walked out the door. Liza stood there in tears as Andy and Arial held and comforted her.

The rest of her visit was spent in sorrow. She not only felt as if she was taking everything from the person she considered her grandpa but had the feeling it would be the last time she would see him. She left the next day after saying goodbye to everyone. The trip back was the longest she ever had.

Chapter 35

The Passing

Again, Liza threw herself into her studies, and things got back to normal. She felt she had to keep busy and keep her mind on school to keep from thinking about her grandpa.

At the farm, Jean and Scott were busy preparing things for visitors. Their plan was to have the place up and running as soon as Liza completed her schooling and set up her practice at the farm as planned. She not being there as a therapist did not prevent them from the other activities the foundation was established for.

Posters were placed around town, and Andy helped spread the word that any child wanting a time for relaxation and association with animals was invited to take advantage of the place free of charge. The original sign that said "Private Property, keep out" was replaced by one that said "All Welcome in Peace and Love." At first, few took advantage or the invitation, partially due to parents' past conception of the property.

In time, however, young students walking home from school began to drop by out of curiosity. Some became regulars, and they brought others. Jean always had cookies and goat's milk for the children. Roger, who spent his time on the porch swing, especially when children were present, would entertain them with his stories. They would join him on the swing or gather around, with them fixed on his presentation. The younger ones, especially the girls, loved to play with his long white beard. At times he was asked if he was Santa Claus, to which he always responded, "Santa Claus is the spirit of love we should all have and celebrate." He had to be careful not to discourage those who still believed in him and yet not insist his existence with those who no longer believed.

Annie became another popular attraction on the farm. And she loved the attention. Some of the older children even volunteered to learn to milk her. Some took to it enthusiastically and made a point of being there during milking time. There was never a shortage of volunteers, and a little spilt milk only led to laughter and part of the fun of the activity. Jean always supervised, but only to give guidance and prevent any activity that could cause harm.

The chickens were also popular, especially with the girls. They had to add more chairs for them to sit on while they held and petted them. Some of the regulars soon picked out their chicken, and attachments were developed.

Overall, you could say the sanctuary was a success. Attendance was not now, a few after school and more on weekends. It kept everyone busy. Andy would drop by once in a while to assist, and that encouraged the children even more. It was exciting to meet the mayor. Parents came to believe if he supported the place, it must be all right and safe. Some of the parents even came out to check the place out, with a few coming out as a family outing. They saw how happy their children were as they joined Roger on the swing with smiles, watching their children running and playing and having fun.

Roger was enjoying himself. He and his place once feared by children who now, as adults, sat by him comfortably, enjoying their children having fun. He wanted to get up and play with them, but his health prevented it. Even so, at times he became so excited he would stand up and, with the help of his staff, head for the steps to the porch. Scott and Jean had to stop him, but when they didn't see him in time, the children would support him as best they could until he was helped back to the swing by an adult. He became Grandpa to all the children, and Jean finally got her wish of a big family of children. Scott, who had to oversee everything, also got his wish to be in charge. He no longer worked for someone else; he was his own boss. He liked making decisions, even though he was most often the one to perform the task involved. He was proud of himself, something he had struggled with his whole life. He felt he had never been in charge, and now he was.

Everything was going well. Roger seemed to perk up with the visitors, especially the children. Soon they didn't think of his health as a problem. He had taken his medication and, according to the doctor, was out of danger or a relapse.

One morning as Scott came in the back door, as he did every morning, he said, "Grandpa, it is time to get up." He never came too early because they allowed him to sleep in. Scott was the one to arrive first at the farm since he quit his job, and Jean stayed home to clean up after breakfast and do needed housework. But he got no response. That was not unusual since Grandpa slept soundly. However, when he entered the bedroom to rouse him, he got no response as he gently shook and again called to him. Still no response, and upon closer observation, he realized Grandpa had passed in the night.

At first he was in shock. He had to call someone, but who? Should he call his wife, Liza, Andy, the doctor, or 911? In the end he called Andy, knowing he knew who to contact, and that would allow him to call his wife. "Honey, I have some bad news—" He didn't have a chance to say anything more.

"No, no, don't tell me." She quickly set the phone down and ran out the door. She didn't bother to grab a jacket or anything else. In fact, she ran all the way to the farm and burst into the door. "Where is he?" She was in hysterics as her husband grabbed her as she came through the door.

"He is in his bed. He passed peacefully in his sleep."

"I want to see him!" she yelled.

"Calm down, there is nothing we can do for him. I've called Andy.

He is making all necessary arrangements. All we can do is wait."

"I still want to see him. He is my grandfather, and it is my responsibility to take care of him."

Scott knew there was nothing he could do to prevent her from entering the bedroom, so he took her into his arms and led her into the bedroom. She knelt down at the side of the bed and gently smoothed his hair back. Then she leaned over and kissed him on the forehead. With tears streaming down her face, she said, "I love you, Grandpa." Then she turned to her husband. "We have to make him presentable. Help me get him dressed."

"Jean, there is nothing we can do. The people coming to pick him up will know what to do, and they are not expecting someone in a suit. They should be here anytime now. Let's go wait in the kitchen at the table."

"No, I will stay by his side. I don't want to leave him alone."

At that time, Andy rushed in and went straight to the bedroom, where Jean got up and gave him a big hug. Neither said a word. Andy then turned to Scott and said, "The ambulance is right behind me. We need to give them room to do their job. Let's retire to the kitchen and move the table so they can get through."

"I'm not going to leave him."

Just then three attendants from the ambulance came into the house. Andy, who had moved to the kitchen, indicated to the bedroom, and he and Scott moved the table out of the way. Scott then returned to the bedroom and took hold of his wife's shoulders and said, "Come, honey, let's give them room to do their job."

"But I want to go with him."

"They will be taking him to the morgue. It is not a place for you." Then he nodded to the attendants to do their job. And they moved out of the bedroom. "I'm sure Liza is in classes by now, but we should call the Wilsons to have them call us as soon as she returns home."

Andy, consoling them both, then cut in, "There is something I need to do." He then went into the shop and came out in about twenty minutes with two wooden plaques, a hammer, and nails. He just walked past them without a word and walked out the back door.

He first went to the corral gate, where he nailed on the first plaque. It was engraved with an image of a goat with the name Nanny inlayed beneath it. The second plaque, he took to the barn. He brought out a ladder from inside and nailed that plaque above the barn door. An image of a chicken was engraved on it with the name Henrietta inlayed below it. Both plaques were made of solid oak with the lettering inlayed in alder, making them stand out.

Jean and Scott had followed him outside and were standing on the porch watching him. When he finished, he joined them. "I have finished Grandpa's last request of me. He told me that upon his death, I was to open the cabinet where he kept special projects and follow instructions. When I opened it, I found a hammer and nails, the plaques, and the note with the instructions. I'm not sure why he wanted to wait, or why he wanted me to do it, but it made me feel good doing it, and I have the impression he was trying to tell me something—construction brings more joy than destruction."

The Petersons slowly walked to the corral gate to get a better look. Then walked to the barn and looked up at the plaque there. "They are beautiful," Jean commented. Even after he is no longer here, he puts on the finishing touch."

Her husband then added, "He is here, he will always be here. He is a part of this place."

Jean, still looking up, had a smile on her face and tears in her eyes. "Thank you, Grandpa for everything. Scott is right, you will always be with us and a part or this place."

By this time, the ambulance attendants had finished loading Roger into their vehicle and were driving off. Arm and arm, all three turned and watched them drive away.

Eventually, Andy went back to work, and Scott and Jean gathered themselves together and managed to call the Wilsons. They did not go into specifics but only told them to have Liza call them at the farm as soon as she got home. As usual, children began arriving after school, and, instead of turning them away, they took care of them as usual, knowing that's what Roger would want them to do. The children noticed the absence of the old man in the swing. Their questions were answered with "he is not feeling good today." Neither of them were emotionally prepared to host that day. But they pushed through the best they could. Fortunately, they had few visitors, and when the last left at five, they posted a sign at the end of the driveway that read "Closed until further notice."

As usual, Jean busied herself cleaning up the house. Scott took care of the normal daily activities outside. The phone rang just after five thirty, and Jean answered it and told Liza to hold on until she could get her father on the line with her. She rushed outside to get him, and they both rushed back into the house so they could both sit down and talk to her together. They were both hesitant to break the news, but finally, her father broke the silence. "Liza, I want you to make sure you are sitting down. I don't know any other way to tell you other than to tell you straight out. Grandpa passed away last night in his sleep. There was no pain, and he left happy." He heard the phone drop. "Liza, Liza, are you there?"

Liza had been sitting on her bed. When she dropped the phone, she, at first, just sat there in shock. She then collapsed onto the bed, still in silence, and then started to sob in earnest.

Not receiving a response, her mother got on the phone. "Liza, Liza, honey. It is Mother." They could hear her crying over the phone, and that started Jean crying again. "Liza, he loved you so much. Now it's our turn to show our love and respect for him. We need you to come home so we can make arrangements. I need you, we need you"

Although still an emotional mess, Liza's training started to take over, and she finally picked up the phone. "I'll leave as soon as I can."

"No," her father said. "You have had a long day. I don't want you driving all night after a long day. You get some sleep and leave in the morning. There is nothing that can't wait until you get here. We love you, honey. We'll talk when you get home. Get packed, make arrangements needed, and get some sleep. We'll see you tomorrow." He then hung up the phone and turned to his wife who, by now, had calmed down. "There are times we have to grieve, no matter what psychologists say, and I would rather have her do it tonight in bed than driving after dark. The drive home will be much safer after a night of grief and sleep." There was nothing more to do or say until Liza got home, so after finishing duties at the farm, they went home themselves to get something to eat and get a night's sleep themselves.

Chapter 36

Saying Goodbye

The drive home was long. The tears, for the most part, were gone. However, the deep sorrow persisted. When she arrived home early that afternoon, there were the usual hugs, and water began to flow again with all. Without speaking, they all sat down together on the couch where Liza began to ask questions regarding details. They answered as best they could, describing the events of the previous day. Her parents then informed her they were scheduled to go to the hospital morgue to make final arrangements but wanted to wait for her to get home so they could go together. "Let's go now," Liza offered. "I need to see him one last time. I know he would want things taken care of as soon as possible. There is no reason to put it off."

That put everything in motion as Liza had already grabbed her purse and was already putting on her jacket. Her parents had to rush to catch up with her. When they arrived at the hospital, Liza and her parents viewed their grandfather for the last time and, accompanied by more tears, said their goodbyes.

Then came the paperwork. They had been through this before with Nanny. Roger's request for cremation and to be buried next to Nanny was unquestionably to be honored. Again, Andy stepped in to assist in the arrangements over the phone. They felt his aid was not necessary, but it was greatly appreciated and simplified and sped things up. Besides, he was considered family and insisted on being involved. Liza now found she would have to apply her training on grief counseling on herself, and that was harder than she thought.

Liza insisted on visiting the farm when they left the hospital. She had not been there since returning home. When they drove in, she immediately noticed the plaque on the corral gate. "When did this happen?"

"It was one of Grandpa's last surprises. He had been working on them for weeks and left Andy with the instructions to mount them upon his demise."

"Them? Them indicates more than one. Where are the others?"

"Look at the barn," her mother said.

As Liza turned to the barn and saw the second plaque, she began to cry. "They are beautiful. I love them. But why wait to mount them after he died? And why did he ask Andy to do it?"

"Andy has a theory," her mother replied. "You'll have to discuss it with him. I think it is a message to not forget. These were two special friends that will always be a part of this place. They are a symbol of what love can accomplish."

Then she slowly walked to the corral plaque. Her emotions took over as she ran her hands over the engravings. She knew Nanny would always be a part of this place and her. "I love you, Nanny. We were a team, and you will always be in my heart. I'll make you proud of me. Take care of Grandpa. He needs you just as I did. Love you always.

Then she entered the corral and gave Annie a big hug. It was not Nanny, but it was someone who needed love as she did years ago. She then walked to the barn and looked up at the memorial to Henrietta. "Grandpa, you put the perfect finishing touch to this farm. I promise to make you proud and fulfill your dream."

They then proceeded to take care of the normal activities necessary to take care of the farm. Once completed, they then sat down to tackle the task making funeral arrangements. Most directions were dictated already by Roger, but actual arrangements and a guest list had to be taken care of.

Darrell, who had been Roger's executor, called them to make arrangements for the settlement of his will. "Mr. Dobson," Liza responded, "I prefer not to discuss any legal matters until he is placed in his final resting place." Usually, she addressed him only by his first name, which he preferred. But at this point, she felt impressed to handle the legal matters on a professional level.

"Of course," he responded. "I completely understand. We can set a time and place at a later, more convenient date. Again I would like to offer my sincere condolences. He was a very dear friend, and he will be greatly missed by everyone, including many who never new or met him."

"What do you mean by 'even many who never new or met him'?" "That is one of the matters that we will go over at the settlement of the will."

Liza hung up with more questions on her mind. Apparently, Grandpa still had more surprises for them. By this time, it was getting late, and Liza realized she hadn't eaten all day. Her parents guessed as much, so they insisted on going home to prepare a meal and go to bed. Tomorrow would be another day, and apparently, they were in store for more surprises.

The next morning, they got down to business. The time for grieving was over. There was to be no formal memorial service, only a gravesite farewell. They felt a simple phone call to each they wanted to attend would suffice, since everyone was already considered family. Outside of Liza and her parents and Andy and his family, Darrell was the only other to be present. In reality, everyone did not have to be invited; their presence was expected. They only had to be notified of the time, since again, everyone knew the location. Darrell, being the only unadopted family member to attend, nonetheless was Roger's first and oldest friend since he moved here, and you couldn't keep him away if you wanted to.

They were able to arrange for the cremation that afternoon. They had to rush to complete all official documents and, in doing so, were hit with another surprise. Apparently, Andy and he had been working on a special project in secret. When Liza and her parents read the death certificate, they noticed something they thought was a mistake. "They didn't include his complete legal name," Liza remarked to Andy who was, as usual, with them at these times.

"Let me see that," he said. He then took it and looked it over carefully. "I don't see anything wrong."

"But it has his last name as Peterson. That is our last name, not his legal name."

"No, Peterson is his legal last name. You see, he wished to adopt all of you but decided he wanted to be a Peterson. So in reality, you adopted him, and you are officially his family."

"Are you pulling my leg? But how?"

"It took a little legal wrangling, but once we got his last name changed to Peterson, we proceeded to formalize an official adoption of each of you. You know, getting all your records was not an easy project, but he was determined. You will now be burying Roger Peterson, your official grandfather, or great-grandfather, whichever you prefer."

"He did that all for us?"

"He did it for him. He wanted to be a Peterson for years, and we finally made it happen."

Liza turned to her parents, giving them a hug. Despite the fact she thought the tears were over, they came again anyway. But this time, the tears were of joy instead of sadness.

Her father commented, "He always was a man of secrets and surprises. I suspect we haven't seen the last of them."

The actual funeral, or burial, was set for three in the afternoon the next day, which was on a Sunday. Although not affiliated with any organized church, they had attended services at a local church in their neighborhood. Roger had impressed on them that everyone was religious. We all believe in a higher power. Nature itself was a higher power, and the existence of a god was quite possible. Religions throughout the world prayed to a deity in different ways under different names, but it was very possible in reality they were all praying to the same individual.

Liza expressed a strong impulse to attend church services this Sunday before their services for Grandfather. "I think it is a wonderful idea," her mother said. "I think we all could use some meditation after the last couple of days."

The sermon was on "Service to Our Fellow Man." When they arrived home, Liza had a smile on her face. "I can't help thinking Grandpa is still talking to us. That sermon was exactly what he would advise. I'm glad we went. Now I'm ready to go forward, knowing he will always be there to guide and protect us in doing what he wanted us to do."

Chapter 37

Final Farewells

By two thirty, everyone was assembled at the burial site next to Nanny and Henrietta. Although Liza and her parents had discussed an urn for the ashes, Andy informed them a vessel was already arranged for. He had picked up the ashes at the hospital, where they were placed in a decorated wooden box. Another surprise, he had informed Andy of earlier with another note. It was also hidden with the plaques in his secret cabinet. He handed it to Liza. "He had his projects, even to the end."

Liza gently accepted the box with a smile, aimed at Andy but also as an acceptance of another example or Roger's thoroughness and attention to detail.

Present were Liza, her parents, Darrell, and Andy with his mother and wife, Arial, with their young son, Roger.

Liza gently placed the box in the grave, which her father had dug out earlier. They all took turns covering the box with dirt. Surprisingly, Roger had not prepared his own grave marker. He had left that up to his apprentice Scott to do. In fact, Scott insisted on it when Roger mentioned he wanted to make one. Although Scott insisted he do it, he did not want to start on it until after he was gone. He felt it would be improper to do so. Now he planned to delve into it with love and respect. He was going to take his time to make sure it was perfect and meet the standards of the master, his teacher.

When the grave was covered satisfactorily, Liza spoke up, "Grandpa would not want this to be a time of sorrow. He would want us to remember him not only with love but happy memories. I want each to relate something joyful so we can all send him off with smiles and laughter.

"There were so many joyful events we had, but I will only relate one that come to the front of my mind. It was on a sunny afternoon, and I was milking Nanny with some difficulty. She had spilt most of the milk. And to make things worse, words were spoken between Grandpa and I. I ended up pouring what little milk there was in the bucket over his head where he sat in the swing with Mom and Dad."

"I remember that," Jean said. "You got some milk on me too."

"You ran into the house to get a towel to clean up. After the shock, we were all laughing so hard no one paid attention to you trying to clean up," Scott said.

"I was afraid he would get mad. But Grandpa just pulled me in with the rest of you, giving me a big hug and laughing so hard I thought he would pee his pants."

That brought laughter from everyone there. When everyone settled down, Jean cut in, "Grandpa and I, as you know, spent a lot of time alone together, helping around the farm when you were working and Liza in school. To take a break, we had a game we would play. We called it egg toss. We would stand toe to toe with one of us holding an egg. We would then hand the egg to the other person and then each move back one step. After each step, the egg was passed back to the other person. As the distance increased, tossing and catching the egg became more difficult. In time, we got pretty good at it but broke a lot of eggs in the process. Once the egg broke, the game was over. There was no winner. It was just a game to see how far apart we could get without breaking the egg. One day we were doing exceptionally well and were about twenty feet apart and proud of ourselves. I threw the egg with a little more force and, to be honest, with poor accuracy, and it smashed into his face. He immediately fell to the ground. His face was dripping with egg, and I rushed over, thinking something was wrong. He just burst out laughing and pulled me down next to him. I said, 'You have egg on your face.' He just laughed harder. We just laid there, laughing and looking up at the beautiful sky. I finally helped him up and led him into the house, where we cleaned him up. With all the egg on his face, he could hardly see. We again had a good laugh, but the egg toss game came to an end."

Her story brought out mixed responses. There were laughs but some expressions of shock. But in the end, they all smiled and laughed and joked with each other. Andy, the baseball pitcher he was, commented, "Remind me never to pick you for my team if we play baseball." That brought out more laughs as Jean gave him a friendly nudge to the shoulder.

Scott related the time when he was helping Roger weed his garden and couldn't tell the weeds from the vegetables and ended up digging up a lot of the beets. "Roger looked at me and said, 'Looks like we are going to be harvesting weeds. I wonder how good they will taste. Then he said, 'Here, trade hoes with me.' He then took my hoe. And he began digging up the beets. By now I could see he was purposely leaving weeds while digging up the beets. I was in shock. He just turned to me and exclaimed, 'Yup, just as I thought, your hoe is defective. It can't tell a weed from a vegetable.' Even though I was a little shocked, I couldn't help but laugh. He joined me, and we both laughed as we were leaning on our hoes. We continued to weed the garden, and I was more careful. He never got mad at anything, even when I made mistakes in the shop. He just said, 'Learning is the process of making mistakes, and mistakes are only the signs of trying.' I learned a lot from him. Not only the ability to have fun even when things went wrong but about life itself."

Andy spoke up, "I can't agree with you more. I didn't have the opportunity to spend the time with him you three did, but I learned a lot from him. In time, I realized he knew I was the one with the indiscretion with the rock when I was younger. But he never brought it up. It was several years before I was aware of his contribution to my college fund. But again, it never became a topic between us. I came to realize that none of these incidents in his mind were related. All he saw was a child who made a mistake and a family that was struggling.

I now understand his desire for secrecy. He never wanted us to draw a connection. As I said, in his mind, they were not related, and he would never hold a grudge or place blame. He accepted me for who I could become. All I can do now is remember him with a smile and try to pass on what I have learned through his example. It was with a smile every time that he greeted me, and it will be with a smile that I will say goodbye to him for the last time."

Beth, who had taken the baby from Arial, spoke up, "I can't add much to what my son has said, but I now see his wisdom. For one thing, I am now holding a grandchild I am proud to say is his namesake. I am so proud of my son for what he has accomplished and thankful for the guidance and assistance Roger provided. I didn't understand the reasoning behind his strange methods, but, as Andy said, he had his reasons. I learned, when you really care for someone, you don't need words. He was a person of few words but all action. Like Andy said, I will always have a smile on my face when I remember him. Goodbye, Grandpa, you will always be with us, and we will make sure little Roger here will know all about his namesake." That made Andy smile as he leaned over to take his son from his mother's arms.

"Well, I guess that only leaves me," exclaimed the banker. "I could relate many occasions of joy brought about because of Roger. So I guess now is as good a time as any to let you in on another of his secrets. I know you are aware of his part in the park Santa. Well, he went further than that. All those wooden toys and Christmas tree decorations he made in his workshop had other destinations. He refused to deliver them personally. Each Christmas, I became his delivery elf. I don't know if you are aware of it, but we have an orphanage here. And each year, that orphanage received a carload of gifts handmade by the park Santa. But it didn't stop there. Fortunately, or unfortunately, depending how you look at it, my position exposed me to many needy families—some after disasters such as fire, family deaths, or just bad luck.

"It became a partnership that changed my philosophy and outlook on life. I provided information and potential needy families. He was insistent no child should be toyless, especially around Christmastime. Now that torch he intended to pass on to you Scott. He informed me you have become very talented in woodworking and toy making and wished you would carry on the tradition."

"I always wondered what happened to all the items he and I made but really wasn't concerned since we just enjoyed making them. I knew he gave them away but had no idea of the orphanage or the network you both had developed. As far as carrying on that tradition, I would be honored."

"I'm glad to hear that. I will continue to provide potential families, and together, we will continue to make Alderwood a friendly and happy community."

"As mayor," Andy broke in, "I would be honored to assist in any way possible. It sounds like the exact project this community needs. I had no idea Roger was so engaged. But then I have only been mayor for a short time and been involved in other projects."

Darrell spoke up again. "Liza, I think we have gotten a little off track. I am sorry. But when you feel we are finished here, there are other matters I feel obliged to impart to you. I will wait for you at the house when you are ready. So long, my old friend, we made a good team. We will meet again and talk again of fond memories." At that, he turned and walked back down the hill to the house.

After he left, the others just stood there, mostly in silence. Andy and his family were the next to leave. Liza's parents soon left her alone with her thoughts to say her goodbye privately. They joined Darrell at the house where they all went into the kitchen to wait for Liza.

When she finally walked in, she was melancholy and sad as expected, but her training helped. Grieving was essential, but she had spent the last two days doing that. Now it was time to move on. "Now what is this previously unknown information you feel obligated to impart to us?"

"You have been informed of his will and desire to turn this place into a sanctuary for the benefit of those needing emotional support. And that he planned for you to set up an office here using your degree for that purpose, and your family was to become not only overseers but administrators of the foundation funded by public and city funds. But he had set up another foundation."

"What are you talking about, another foundation?" Liza asked.

"You realize he paid off the mortgage on your home?" They all nodded. "You also realize you did not qualify for a loan?"

"But we worked things out," Scott said.

"Not really. Roger backed up your loan. He promised to cover any payment in default. He didn't know you at the time, and you were not the only ones to benefit from his assistance. He would sit down with me, and we would go over applications that were denied by the bank. He would pick out those he felt deserved a break, as he put it. He never based his decision on the financial ability to pay. Like I said, he promised to cover the loans with his own money, essentially setting up a foundation of his assets for the specific purpose to make payments when and if necessary. Although they were bank loans, as the bank owner and manager, we were the only ones aware of them, and I took care of them personally. As of today, your mortgage is the only one paid in full. However, none of the others have fallen into default. Those loans he chose that were rejected by the bank have a better payment record than those the back accepted. He knew, when given the chance, most people down and out, would work hard and sacrifice to get on their feet. Some have struggled greatly, but all have met their payments on time.

"As per my insistence, since he actually financed those loans, he was entitled to some of the interest generated by them. He insisted on not taking one cent in profit, so I have returned it to the foundation I insisted be set up. Some of that money was used to pay off your mortgage, but there is still quite a sum left. It is now up to you to decide what to do with those funds."

"I had no idea," Scott said. "But why us?"

"Like I said, he made choices on instinct. He didn't know you. You were just one he chose. It was only a coincidence that brought you together. At the time of his meeting with Liza and for months after, he wasn't even aware you were one of the recipients of his generosity. As Andy pointed out, he did not let an event affect another. He kept everything separate."

"How much are we talking about?" Liza inquired.

"I don't have the exact figures, but it runs close to a hundred thousand. You have the option to turn it over to our foundation here at the farm or elect to do something else with it."

"We don't want any of that money. Our foundation is adequately funded. Why can't you use that money to pay off or down the other outstanding loans or finance more?"

"I wouldn't pretend to have the insight Roger had in picking out worthy recipients. So I wouldn't suggest that. But funding the mortgages was the original intent of the trust, so that is a distinct possibility."

"I think that is what we should do then. If you could spread it out evenly and draw up the papers, we will gladly sign them. Would that take care of things and nullify the foundation, or trust, as you call it?"

"I'm sure it can be arranged. To be honest, I didn't know how I was going to take care of it once I was gone. I'll get started on it right away. Do you want to know the parties involved?"

"No. Keep it the way Grandpa intended."

"Very well, then. It was a good service, just like he would have wanted. Again I offer my condolences. I'll be in touch." He gave them each a hug and walked out the door.

"I have a grave marker to make," Scott commented. He then stood up from the large table he and Roger made since the kitchen table was too small to accommodate them all and headed for the workshop. Jean took on her usual task of cleaning and straightening up the house. Liza went outside to take care of the animals. There was nothing left to say, and they all needed alone time to evaluate their feelings and the future.

Roger had laid a course and a role and purpose for each of them. Now it was up to each to fulfill their callings. They each looked forward to their positions and realized they now were in a position to do something they were looking for their whole lives. Jean would have a large family of children she wanted. Scott was able to use his creative skills and was his own boss with no financial worries. Liza was on course to be a counselor for children with challenges she herself faced. They all realized helping others led to the ultimate reward of happiness.

Liza returned to school, and her parents again opened the sanctuary. Darrell launched into the distribution of the trust funds and drawing up papers to dissolve it. Andy returned to his responsibilities as mayor and reveled in his new role as a father. He continued to make appearances at the farm just to see how things were going and see if there was anything he could do to help.

Chapter 38

Life Goes On

The next year was busy for all. Liza was able to concentrate on school. They had to hire more help to accommodate the increase of visitors at the sanctuary. It so happened their new help was Arial's younger brother, who had returned from college with a degree in social services. That led to Arial visiting with her and Andy's son, Roger, on a frequent basis. He was now almost two and loved playing with Annie.

Scott managed to complete the grave maker. They waited for Liza to be there during one of her visits to place it at the grave site. In fact, everyone that was at the funeral, except Darrell, made a point to be there. Everyone commented on how beautiful it was, and Scott took great pride in making it. Engraved on the plaque was "Roger Peterson, beloved grandfather and teacher." The dates of his birth and death were also included. They showed his age at passing to be ninety-nine, two months short of reaching one hundred.

Darrell managed to anonymously distribute the funds in Roger's trust to the outstanding mortgages involved. This automatically dissolved the fund. Liza's signature was required in these procedures, which she was anxious to do on one of her visits home.

After graduation, Liza returned home with an official license to practice. She had a master's in child psychology and speech therapy. She was licensed as a speech-language pathologist. She was anxious to begin her practice. Her parents had set up her office in the living room, giving her the room necessary to help patients. It gave them room to walk around as well as room for the recliner they could relax on. The desk was Roger's with his computer and printer on it. The recliner was also his. Liza added a few computer accessories and file cabinets but felt most comfortable the way it was when her Grandpa was there at the large table, which allowed her to spread out paperwork when needed.

Within a few months, Liza's appointments became overwhelming. Her mother ended up becoming her secretary, making and scheduling appointments. She kept Liza informed of her schedule but also made sure she took time to eat and also made sure to schedule time for breaks. She also made sure no one entered the house during sessions, to provide the required privacy. Jean worked from the bedroom, where she had her desk and phone. The door was closed when Liza had a session to allow privacy. Otherwise, it was always open.

The two men outside were also overwhelmed. Scott could only spend time in the shop after visiting hours and on Sunday when the center was closed. Although Liza only took patients on weekdays, she made herself available anytime in emergencies. On Saturdays, she would help out outside with the children. Fortunately, parents with children in counseling would also help with other visitors while waiting for their child. In many cases, they had other children with them, so it became nature.

Again the need for more help became apparent. Austin, Arial's brother, was basically running the show outside. He was having the time of his life but was overwhelmed. Since they were giving out Christmas tree decorations to all the children, Scott knew he had to spend more time in the shop. He still had the orphanage presents to think of. He didn't know how Roger managed to keep up. Of course, he didn't have a yard full of visitors.

Darrell, who had resorted to complete retirement, now that he didn't have any more of Roger's finances to manage, suggested his grandson help them out. He felt he needed guidance. He was not a bad boy but lacked direction and felt college unnecessary. Coming from a banking family, he had become accustomed to having everything handed to him. He didn't have a job and felt no incentive to get one. He liked his grandfather, so with a little convincing and working things out with the Petersons, they decided to try him out on a voluntary basis with no set hours. Scott, who was in charge of outside activities, was reluctant, but Liza, being the therapist she was, convinced her father to give him a chance. As it turned out, Adam, named after his father, enjoyed associating with the children and animals. When Liza got a break, she would sit down with him on the swing and talk to him informally. She was very good at her job, and they developed a close relationship. He ended up showing up on a regular basis, and they eventually put him on the payroll. His grandfather was so impressed he even showed up to help once in a while. Probably just to be with his grandson.

They still had the regular activities taking care of the animals and maintaining the grounds. Those activities were a seven-day-a-week job. Jean and Scott were there every day, but for Liza, it was her home. She stayed in the bedroom that, during the day, was used by her mother as an office. Adam and Austin shared yard work for the most part but, on occasion, visiting children chipped in. It became a community gathering place, and Liza's counseling, in a couple of years, became recognized and raved about. Her college professors, whom she kept in contact with, held her in high esteem.

The success of not only her counseling but the retreat as a whole impressed others throughout the state and beyond. Other communities invited her to open a similar operation in their communities. She refused, saying she was not interested. It was a center run under a tax-exempt foundation supported by funds from the city and private contributions. Since it was nonprofit, there was no charge for services. And she doubted it would work in another community. In reality, she felt it was a success because it was Roger's place, the farm, and no other place would work as well.

One Sunday, they received a visit from Bob, the mayor when Roger moved in. He was instrumental in Roger's ability to purchase and develop the property. He was along in years by now, and they hadn't had much contact with him since he retired and Andy took over his position. "I just wanted to visit and see for myself the talk of the town. Although, through the years, I have lost touch with my old friend and have neglected to build a relationship with you. My health has suffered lately, but I just wanted to come over and tell you how grateful I am for what you have done for the community. You may not know, but Roger and I spent many hours to get this place livable. Now look what you have done with it. Who could have dreamed it possible considering his personality then? You did wonders with him and have done wonders with this place. He was indeed an amazing man, and I just wanted to stop by to let you know how proud I am of you, and say goodbye to a dear friend. Would you mind if I visited his grave? It would mean a lot to me."

Jean was the first to respond, "Of course, I'll take you there. We are all so thankful for your assistance in obtaining this property. You are welcome anytime." Since it was fall and a little chilly outside, she grabbed her sweater and escorted him out the door. She then led him to the burial site.

"You know a miracle has happened here," he commented. "Once this was the most feared, disliked, and misunderstood place in town. It is now one of the most popular. I remember when it was a place of fear and hate. Now everyone considers it a place for healing and love. Yes, it is nothing short of a miracle, and I'm proud to feel I had a small part in it. Would you mind if I could be alone to say my goodbyes to an old friend in private? As I said, my health prevented me from visiting when he departed, but I do want to show my respects before I join him. I can find my way out when I am finished." When Jean returned to the house, she related what Bob had related to her, and added, "I never realized how close he was to Grandpa. He was talking about how glad he will be to see him again."

After her parents left that evening, Liza sat at her desk, going over some sessions and making notes. She was deep in thought, going over what Mr. Wells had said, and realized how many lives her grandfather had touched and affected. Many of those would never know. She spoke out loud, "To some people, he was Santa Claus, others a guardian angel, and others a savior. I've heard some religions teach there are prophets, such as Moses, who never experienced death. They claim they walked the earth to this day. Others claim there are aliens who created us and are still here watching over us. But I don't care who he was, or where he came from. He was, and will always be, my grandfather and will live in my heart forever."

EPILOGUE

Quite often we never know the affects of an act of kindness. Who, or how, is an undetermined factor. But you can be assured there will be an effect on someone at some time. This book and the characters are fictional, but the feelings are real to many people today and I am convinced almost everyone can relate to one of the characters. Writing the book, I became each and every character; feeling their emotions as if I were them. I would hope readers are able to do the same, because it is our emotions that guide our lives.

ABOUT THE AUTHOR

Keith is married and living in Sandy, Utah. He loves to travel and is fascinated with ancient history and the study of it. He is interested in not only past cultures but modern cultures as well. The study of the people and places throughout the world is important for a better, peaceful world. He has a love for animals but prefers them in the wild in their natural habitat. He strongly believes in a harmonious world that includes the balance of nature of all plants and animals, with humans being part of that animal kingdom and cycle of life and not controllers. We as humans must learn to not only get along but be there to help each other without prejudices. These feelings and beliefs have prompted Keith to volunteer at senior centers and make, in his workshop, small wood projects which he gives away, especially at Christmas.

www.ingramcontent.com/pod-product-compliance
Lightning Source LLC
Chambersburg PA
CBHW051509120626
46551CB00012B/847